WISDOM FROM THE DASHAVATARA

Leadership Lessons on Start-ups

PRACHI GARG

Om EDGE
An Imprint of Om Books International

First published in 2026 by

Om EDGE An Imprint of Om Books International

Corporate & Editorial Office
A-12, Sector 64, Noida 201 301
Uttar Pradesh, India
Phone: +91 120 477 4100
Email: editorial@ombooks.com
Website: www.ombooksinternational.com

Sales Office
107, Ansari Road, Darya Ganj,
New Delhi 110 002, India
Phone: +91 11 4000 9000
Fax: +91 11 2327 8091
Email: sales@ombooks.com
Website: www.ombooks.com

ISBN: 978-93-6395-620-9

Printed in India

10 9 8 7 6 5 4 3 2 1

Prachi Garg is a celebrated author, motivational speaker, entrepreneur, and technology leader. Her six bestselling books—*Superwomen, Supercouples, Supersiblings, The Legends of a Start-up Guy, Startup Secrets from the Ramayana, and Ganesha's Global Startup*—have left a lasting impact on the Indian startup ecosystem. These titles consistently top charts across major bookstores and continue to inspire emerging entrepreneurs and changemakers.

She is the founder of ghoomophiro.com, a pioneering women-led travel platform that has been featured on CNN, *The Hindu*, *Indian Express*, *Business Today*, and more. Prachi has been recognized among the top ten Indian women who made it big online, and her entrepreneurial voice has won accolades such as the Indian Achievers' Award, the Economic Times Inspiring Leadership in Technology recognition, and the Adgully Women Disruptor of the Year in Technology award.

In 2025, *Femina* magazine honored her as a Changemaker, acknowledging her transformative work at the intersection of technology, entrepreneurship, and women's empowerment.

Professionally, Prachi is a technology leader at Adobe, where she plays a key role in driving digital transformation through Artificial Intelligence. Her focus includes AI-powered customer journeys, data-driven product strategies, and the responsible deployment of AI. She is also actively involved in mentoring startups and policy research on the future of AI in airspace, low-altitude economy, and sustainable innovation.

A prolific speaker and writer, Prachi shares her insights on entrepreneurship, women in tech, and AI leadership at global forums. Her thought pieces have appeared on platforms like YourStory, Entrepreneur, and various vernacular publications.

Academically, she is a distinguished alumna of Miranda House, University of Delhi, with a postgraduate degree in

Computer Science. She holds an MBA from Great Lakes Institute of Management and has completed a Leadership Course at the Said Business School, University of Oxford.

To the quiet dreamers and bold builders, those who believe in beginnings. And to my family—for being my why, always.

Contents

Chapter 1

Meeting Manav

The aroma of stale chai clung to the air in Manav's small, one-room apartment, a testament to his sleepless night. Dawn crept in, a bleary and indifferent intruder, but sleep remained elusive. He sat hunched by the window, arms wrapped around his knees, a meagre barricade against a world that felt increasingly hostile. Empty teacups, monuments to his restless vigil, formed a semicircle around him.

What kept him awake? Was it the need for caffeine, or something deeper—a thought, a memory, a decision lurking in the shadows, refusing to be faced in the light of day? His bloodshot eyes reflected a heavier weight than mere insomnia. He had questions. A reckoning and A shift that no amount of caffeine could suppress. Life hadn't been kind lately, but this night felt different. As though everything he believed in was quietly slipping out from under him. The silence around him throbbed, louder than any noise. And in that moment, staring out at a world that kept moving without him, Manav felt a strange pull toward reflection, a yearning for change, for a new identity—maybe… reinvention.

A single, tattered calendar hung on the wall, its surface marred by red circles and frantic notes, especially jarring across the last three months. The reason? A lot! Manav's world had turned upside down when the coronavirus pandemic hit the world. In the beginning, just like everyone else, he had thought it was a media panic and things would all disappear after the trend faded or something else came up to attract the world's attention. He, like so many others, had been wrong—a truth that landed squarely on his shoulders when his branch shut down, leaving him unemployed just two months into the infamous lockdown. Although he was not alone, and many people around him had been left abandoned just like him, there was no comfort in company. Especially because he knew that it was not a normal situation, and it was not like he could simply apply to other places and get a job easily. The crisis was hitting hard across sectors, and it would take a miracle for him to get a job immediately.

However, Manav was not one of those people who spend their time mulling over dead grass. He was a man of action and believed in solutions. He knew that somewhere in this crisis, there had to be a silver lining that was meant to bring him an opportunity.

The memory of the old woman who had come asking him for a loan just a week before he was fired rose to the surface as Manav watched his last cup of tea grow cold. The old lady had been trying to set up a business by setting up a shop at her house. As a humanitarian, Manav was tempted to approve her loan.

After all, she had been aspiring to stand on her own feet, with the help of a son who was just a high-school graduate. But as a banker, this was an open-and-shut case.

This was a classic piece of liability that the bank could not afford to carry. A few years ago, Manav would still have been naive enough to raise a request. But now, with experience, he had learned what dreams to nip in the bud and which ones to allow to grow. "Amma, I have already told you there's nothing I can do about this." Manav's frustration was not even shrouded anymore. But it was not directed at the poor old and ignorant woman, but at himself for not being able to do anything for her. The irony of business economics was that it favoured those who needed it the most.

Manav had joined this sector because he had a love for numbers, for economics. He wanted to get to the core of financial understanding. Even as a child, he would always be asking his father about the sales and purchases at his little grocery shop.

"How much will you need to sell to make sure you can buy more?" He would pester his father with the most innovative and detailed questions for someone his age.

"Of course, getting into the banking sector is the best way I see for you," his teacher had advised him back in school when he had sought counselling in his final year.

But this was not all that Manav wanted. He had slugged long and hard to crack the banking exam. He had listened to the not-so-pleasant 'mentoring' of his seniors and, more importantly, he had scavenged through the thicks and thins of small businesses, the economics of loans and repayment.

In all of this, he had learnt about the variations of success and, more importantly, the variations of failure. In the last 5 years, Manav had seen people from all walks of life come to ask him for business loans. Of course, these are small businesses. After all, what mammoth opportunities would await the explorers of the small town of Vaikuntha, a small habitat in Northern India, where even online deliveries had only now started knocking on the business door.

But it was not that the population was not aspirational or hardworking. It was just a mix of politics, generations of underprivileged circumstances, and neglect that had left the town far behind in financial growth and business opportunities, which had in turn led to a low standard of living, education, and healthcare.

This, however, had not stopped its citizens from exploring various avenues of success. Every once in a while, an Icarus would fly into nearby cities, or the capital of the state, witness some fascinating marvel of a mall, a fancy salon, or even a cafe, and bring back dreams to build their little utopia in Vaikuntha.

Now, thinking back on all of his observations, himself unemployed, Manav was moved to think about all the men and women who had been unemployed or who had been in the process of building their businesses, or even those who had been struggling to keep their businesses alive. He could think back and recall most of the cases. Most of the time, he would get a loan request for a small hotel proposition, shopping complexes, for starting a school, sometimes, a hostel for NGO workers (since the town's low-income grade made it a hotspot for NGO interventions). Every so often, however, there'd be requirements for someone setting up a small boutique, an arts curation, or a dairy.

These were the kind of prospects that Manav would put his bet on. Not because they were going to succeed. But because they displayed a promise of breaking the bonds and exploring the unknown. "That's what I call being ambitious," Manav would say to his colleague, Ved, during lunch breaks.

They would often discuss their experiences throughout the day, share mutual frustrations about their boss, and talk about ideas that brewed in their cluttered minds. "If you have stepped away from the lines that have been drawn by generations before you, your life has true meaning. Otherwise, you have not lived for yourself."

Manav felt very passionate about this. One would argue about the originality and genuineness of his inspiration. After all, which artist or mentor or founder had he met that had built such crazy ideas in his head? He was, after all, a progeny of the same set of learning, same small-town ideologies, and exposure as the rest of the people around him.

What made him think so differently then? This was another itch that Manav kept scratching time and again... to understand what he was doing, had done and was going to do that made him stand above and beyond the circle of middle-class ants around him, who were all struggling to get a steady job, eat three meals a day, watch television and buy groceries that cost almost the same amount, every week.

There were times when Manav felt a jolt of a sinking feeling, the one you feel when you suddenly reach the edge of a cliff and realise that the drop is a massive one. "That's how large the gap is between me and my friends, Ved, apart from you."

Manav lived in a city where hardly anyone left, but also hardly anyone read, explored, or aspired. Amidst all of this, he felt a drastic loss of connecting and stimulating conversations. Well, this had not been technically true. There was one other person whom Manav had relied on for the greater part of his young life. His childhood friend and confidant, Satrupa, had been working right here in Vaikunth.

Despite being a topper and deserving of a lot of opportunities in the big world outside, Satrupa had been forced to take up a small-time job as a newspaper reporter in Vaikuntha itself because of her sick mother, after having worked only a year outside in a big media house.

Now that she was back, Manav and Satrupa had touched base again and started interacting in a friendly, stuck in the same fish-bowl kind of way that two people with big dreams feel like. They had not thought of each other with a perspective much beyond platonic friendship, and simply because they could relate with one another, it helped them to stick together. After all, there was not much of a social life!

Not only was Manav stuck in his social life, but seemed to have reached a wall as far as his professional growth was concerned. Initially, Manav had been very excited about learning all about risk analysis and capital investments. Even when he still had the job, he would challenge himself by drawing graphs of the business loans that got approved by his superiors, monitor their growth, and assess whether or not he succeeded in analyzing them correctly.

With time, Manav had also been allowed to make independent decisions on small business loans, albeit the ones that posed very little risk. But he had been a keen observer, and there was not a single business in Vaikunth that he was not aware of. Manav enjoyed this observation, made a project out of figuring out the parameters that make a business fail and succeed, at least in terms of finances. But what impressed him the most was the innovation and ambition with which people in the small town continued their experiments and endeavours in the universe of entrepreneurship.

All these moments came clouding back into his memory when he remembered the fate of the old woman who would not be getting any loan approvals now, as the financial situation had worsened. He remembered his conversation with the old lady who had been sitting expectantly, waiting for a miracle to happen. It had been frustrating for him to say no to her. And in the initial phase of her application, he had genuinely tried all possible means to make her application a strong one, an application that could have the slightest hope of being approved, so he could at least make a case with his seniors.

"Amma, it would be easier for you to raise funds if you ask friends and well-wishers. I don't think the bank policies would be in your favour here." Manav had taken a deep breath in before giving a categorical but soft blow of rejection, in one of the earlier calls.

Some of his clients still called him to follow up and to get support, because he had always been so kind and helpful to them. Manav had been scanning the scenario in the rest of the world, and especially evaluating the Indian scenario, and understood now that almost everything would be turning online.

"Looks like this online space is here to stay," Satrupa said. Her office had also turned to most news collection and display to online media, turning to more online presence than print, and can see the impact happening daily.

"Yes, I think e-commerce is going to be the next big market, and if there's anything to be done for ourselves and for the people who are worst hit by the lockdown crisis." Manav was speaking from a context of his habits that had changed immensely ever since the lockdown.

He had been exploring the internet and looking at the trend of how a lot of services were turning online and customising their services. This was exactly how he had found his mantra of survival during his time of turmoil.

It was something Manav had been working on in the last few months. He had chanced upon a meditation channel online while researching for a massage and meditation model he had read about. Stumbling from one link to another, he was eventually led to this channel, which offered a free breathing and meditation guide. Always the explorer, Manav had often contemplated what the world of meditation was all about. Was it a journey to the inner world, or was it simply a mirage of social reputation created by those fancy people who like to smell like incense and wear white, smiling like hippies?

The more Manav excavated his own experiences with meditation, the deeper he found himself wanting to go. Better focus, deeper sleep, and more patience were some of the superficial changes he started observing in himself within the first month of practicing. Perhaps it was that breathing technique that had prompted him to hold on to his patience and talk empathetically to the old lady sitting before him.

Ever since the loss of his job, Manav had been meditating deeper and longer. The more he delved deeper into retrospection, the more he became aware of the world around him. And it helped him connect the dots from all of his experiences in the past to see how they fit into his present and future.

But it was not just these changes that regular meditation had brought him. Of late, Manav had been feeling as though someone was wiping the virtual screen in front of the eyes of his mind. It felt to him that the screen had been foggy and perhaps shaded all this while, without him even realising that he was not being able to see things.

But now, every time he woke up from a deep session of meditation, he felt that he could see things clearly, his life and its goal, its meaning, felt clearer. And he was able to look at things from a fresh perspective. You know how little things culminate into a larger result? Like single flowers making a bouquet, instruments making an orchestra, or people making an organisation? Manav was watching little changes that were beginning to reform his judgement, reactions, and later, as he would realise, even his actions.

In the last few sessions, Manav had been experiencing a very strong push from his subconscious mind, as though it had come alive and was trying to talk to him. A voice inside his head, that he had only very faintly recognised in the beginning, had become quite loud and vocal now and was beginning to appear even in his dreams, probing and poking at his thoughts like a curious historian with old building remains. It was this voice that sometimes appeared in his dreams like a person, sometimes like a bird, a tortoise, a lion, or several other forms and shapes, all telling him to take control of his life and follow the true path.

"You're more than this," it kept repeating into his consciousness like an echo in a deep and endless gorge. Manav had a growing feeling inside his head that he was about to do something radical and borderline questionable. Something that was going to change the way he looked at the world and the way the world looked at him.

All of this was revolving in the background of his thoughts as he spoke to the same old woman when she called him for a follow-up.

"Oh, aunty, you don't know this yet! I don't work there anymore..." Manav stopped himself before spreading any more words of misery. He knew that telling her about the crisis would only make her a lot more nervous.

Instead, he decided to tell her that she had a better chance of raising funds from people around her, not even realising he was setting the innovative wheel in motion.

"How am I ever going to be able to spread the word?" The woman had a genuine concern.

Manav had, over the years, learnt to somewhat shield himself against the disappointment and frustration of turning down loans to those who needed it the most. But this question he couldn't, he wouldn't forget, and it kept playing in his head several times over.

If only there was something he could do for the old woman and all the desperate, aspiring, unfortunate loan seekers, business developers, entrepreneurs, NGO workers, who sought help, who needed to reach an audience to raise money, but ironically did not have the money to be able to reach an audience. Perhaps, this was his wake-up call.

"Amma, here is my number. Give me a week. Please get in touch with me after that. I will try my best to come up with alternative ways for you to raise money," he told the old woman.

It was almost as if something else had taken over Manav's consciousness and was driving his words, his actions, and even his thoughts, as he told the woman to hang on for just a little bit. "I will show you a way out."

In that little act of extending his help, breaking his own rules, and deciding to act, Manav had already taken the first steps to the change he was about to bring. One of these days, he was called over to the office to complete some formalities. Rushing memories came back to him as he shut down his system for the day, assessing his actions in his head, while mechanically handing over all record files to the storekeeper, dishing out the key to his bike, Manav was already drafting his plan of action for the next steps.

A couple of decisions were made that night. First, he was going to do something about the frustration he felt about his professional crisis. Second, he was going to take some action to help cases of rejected loans for people who deserved a second chance in life. He was going to act upon his frustration about not doing anything meaningful and lucrative with his capacity.

And third, he was going to work his brains off figuring out how to blend his first decision with his second decision.

It was for sure that Manav was going to start working to build an enterprise for himself. But nowhere did the rules say that an entrepreneur cannot, in effect, build an enterprise that can serve the larger good, be a support system for those in need, and still build a successful, sustainable, and scalable business model.

In his head, that night, Manav had already drafted a proposal letter in his head. He had picked up and learnt everything he could absorb from the bank, and now, it was time to step out of his comfort zone and put his dreams over a decade into action. He knew it was not going to be easy. He was already looking into the chaos of his mind to hear his voice of guidance, to tell him what the next steps should be. The decision had been made. The tough part was over. Now he had to put all his energy, experience, and efficiency into building a plan, a product, or a possibility.

He was sure he was going to need a lot of help starting the next morning. He knew he was also going to hear a lot of pushback from his family, friends, and colleagues. He could already hear the questions in his head. "Who is going to marry you?" His mother would ask. "Do you have a treasure hidden somewhere that will fund your business?" His friends would whip out taunts. He was already preparing his list of answers, building logic in his head, imagining the words he would use to break the news, the people he would reach out to for guidance, connections, and funds.

But as Manav switched on his meditative podcast, he started categorically slowing down his racing mind with each deep breath he took. It was one of the oldest tricks in meditation that he followed religiously. To journey from the body, to the mind, and the breath, that would ultimately lead to his soul. Resolving stronger with each exhalation, Manav turned to his inner voice and did something he did not remember doing in a very long time. He asked the voice, the universe, and anyone listening to help him, really help him, find the right path.

Manav had read a lot many books in the last few months, and many metaphysical philosophers talked about the interlinking of the universe, how every person and situation are related and connected with each other. As Manav slowly sank into his meditation, he was inadvertently sending out an SOS to the world, not even realising that his words, his intentions, were being heard somewhere and help was coming, very soon and very appropriately, in more than one ways, from the sources he could not have even imagined. "I have a feeling this is going to work out just fine, Satrupa," he had told her before sleeping that night. He was determined that there would be no other way!

Moral: It is like man to continue progressing and evolving. If one is listening truly to oneself and one's environment, there are always triggers, drives, and opportunities that prompt one to be better, both as a person as well as a professional. It is therefore necessary to keep a keen eye, with a passionate observation to understand what is going on around you and how best you can either become a part of the growth or be the change maker yourself. Someone, with the right set of skills, observation, and drive, must make a business opportunity. Problems are plenty, waiting on a platter to be picked up and solved, making it the duty and opportunity of an entrepreneur to make the best of it.

Chapter 2

Understanding the Basics

It had been a few days since Manav had last spoken to Satrupa. He had been discussing with her about this new project that had been orbiting around in his head. He was going to try out a small experiment with the small-scale businesses, especially his favourite Amma, whom he had been hell bent on supporting, despite his crisis. He had given her his phone number and had been working on the idea for promoting small-scale businesses. In this reference, he would speak often and in detail with Ved, the only other person who understood Manav's need to take some action.

"Maybe this is what my idea can be all about." He was discussing with Ved. "I don't have to look for something western, aspirational, or even fancy-sounding, right?" Manav was getting the hang of where he wanted to take his idea. One of the most basic fundamentals of his learning in business had been from the mistakes of those around him, making the best of this crisis as a rising opportunity for the online space.

Manav had never tried his hand at business, but he had seen so many people work on it that his second-hand experience had given him the privilege of exercises and insights without actually having to invest and commit mistakes himself. "But don't you think that makes you less involved in these businesses?" Ved was putting out the last of his cigarette after listening to Manav's monologue. He had always been a good friend and guide for Manav, who always came to him for advice and to discuss all his issues.

Ved was like an encyclopaedia of knowledge. There was hardly ever a subject that he did not have content to talk about or throw some light on. Indeed, he was a well-read man, very intelligent and vastly knowledgeable. But he was also very content with his life. Despite the potential of what he could have done, he had become an age-old part of the landscape, like an important piece of literature kept in the library, accessible to all but sought by only a deeply intellectual seeker.

But Ved was a respite for Manav, who needed intellectual stimulation and the right counselling. "You know, that is why I like you so much, Ved," Manav teased him. "You are the only one who questions my thoughts or actions, contradicts my ideas, and tells me about the mistakes I am about to make right to my face." Manav valued his friend's honest and impartial stand, a quality often missing in friends who surround a genius because a peer group is either always too scared of the smart leader to contradict them, or is only trying to be in the good books by agreeing with their every nod and grunt.

"But this time, you are wrong in disagreeing with me," Manav started with his signature charming smile, as though he knew exactly how to lead the conversation. "It is not that I am not involved enough in these businesses, Ved. I enjoy the vantage point of being a neutral observer and can easily see what decisions and actions are positively or negatively affecting a business." He did have a very fair point. How often had the world seen great potential in business only to be lost because entrepreneurs couldn't keep a dispassionate head on their shoulders and make decisions without the interference of fear, risk, or emotional bias?

Along with all the professional flux, Manav was also undergoing some personal storm. In the last couple of months, Satrupa and he had been talking a lot more often, about a lot more things than just platonic empathy. Ever since Manav had realized how significant a part she had become in his life, he had been dying for Satrupa and Ved to connect and get to know each other. After all, these were the two people whom he could talk to. And strictly from a professional perspective, it would make a lot of sense and make life easier if they could brainstorm together. With this in mind, he finally connected the two over a video call, after all, that's what you could do during the lockdown.

It's not like Manav could take Satrupa out on a date or anything! He shyly introduced Ved and Satrupa. "While we're all stuck individually in our homes, disconnected from the world, I thought it would be a good opportunity to connect you two, since I end up spending a lot of time discussing with you individually, I thought why not do it together and save some time!"

Ved was visibly happy and relieved to see this. He had guessed for a while that Manav had someone in his life, simply because a lot of what he had been talking about these days sounded different. And the only way Manav would have a strong enough influence to affect his conversations was if the source was someone close enough to affect him emotionally.

"Well, I don't care if you're saving time or daylight; I know for a fact that I am being spared a lot of headaches and boredom to have someone to listen to your rants!" Ved joked, and Satrupa gave him a virtual high-five!

Manav was secretly happy to see that the two were getting along well. He felt a breeze of relief knowing that he could now plan his next steps more openly and efficiently with the duo, whom he planned to pitch for partnership. Manav was also simultaneously building a case to talk to people across his network, including his bank and ex-colleagues, to see if they could help in any way.

Despite the way in which he was let go, his relationship with his boss was still surprisingly very cordial, and there was a lot of mutual respect, and frankly, benefit in keeping in touch and helping each other out. His branch still relied on him for a lot of customer relations since he had one of the best ratings in the region.

Because of this, his ex-boss still engaged with some consultancy work with Manav, asking him to follow up on some clients, attend some virtual meetings or make presentations because Manav was one of the most efficient and presentable persons to lead the face of the branch, which was otherwise counted among the last few in the region. Except for when it came to creative implementations, which were essentially led by Manav.

In all of the last couple of months, when our rising star, or a star about to sink, depends on whether you like to see a glass half full or half empty, had been planning on contacting different people for his ideas, there was an announcement at the bank about a financial convention with a core of startup investments and this lured Manav into contacting his ex-boss to attend it. "This is going to be my chance to network with people, send out some words, sniff some possibilities."

He knew anyway that there was no one else who was able enough to represent the branch online and prepare a solid presentation to speak about the ideas. This was the least he could do to tap into the opportunity. What is the whole point of being with an organisation for so many years if I have not built some good faith to carry forward?" Ved agreed. The duo had often been asked to represent the branch because they were young and talented minds, which loosely translated to 'could speak English and handle technology'.

"Not that I mind, playing along, Manav," Ved was coming to a point. Even though he had no intentions of quitting his job, he was determined to help Manav out in his adventures. He cared for his eclectic friend a tad more than he would care to admit. Although whenever Manav would tease him about it, he argued that he liked to hover, only to see what Manav's adventures led him to. "I want to be there when you make that epic fall. It will be quite a laugh, I am sure," Ved laughed. The larger purpose, of course, was for them to learn mutually. And in each of their interactions, the duo played their parts, complementing each other's ideas and actions.

Even in this situation, when Manav was building ideas about what he could do for the convention, Ved and Satrupa were trying to bring his focus back to the specifics. "Remember the next steps. Are you looking for funding? Are you looking for validation of ideas? Or are you scouting for people to help you out? Make sure you have a very clear agenda in your head when you pitch yourself at the convention."

Manav was listening intently, also feeling amazed at the sheer farsightedness of his friends. That was what he truly liked about his power-packed partners. They were both inspired by objective thinking and had a universal thought process. Listening to Satrupa felt like, although she was talking about one thing, there were several layers of meaning to it. If one listened carefully, one could answer several questions. And Ved was a curious and sharp listener, always eager to bounce off ideas and pick up clues from his environment.

Having prepared himself for the convention, apart from the obvious position of being a flag-bearer of the bank branch,

Manav had also been endlessly working on his business idea. Keeping the support system of small-scale or rising businesses as the core of his agenda, Manav has explored the entire universe of possibilities, keeping in mind the essential problem of small-scale businesses.

"At the epicentre lie two issues. One, for small and aspiring businesses, is the lack of promotion, which prevents them from reaching out to potential funders. Because this, they have to be dependent on old-school, non-adventurous sources like our bank." Manav was talking to the dog outside his street. He would generally walk around in the middle of the night, when there was nobody else, and he wouldn't have to maintain social distancing or be afraid of spreading or catching the virus, having conversations with whoever, or, as in this case, whoever came across his path. The dog happily wagged his tail at the fortunate attention of a seemingly non-threatening human. This was more than the encouragement Manav sought in his audience.

"The second is that even if the businesses have the money to bootstrap and kick off, they do not have enough to sustain, let alone scale, even if they may have a business model that has a lot of potential and has already established a proof of concept." Manav was stating the most honest and unfortunate fact about the fate of most small-scale businesses. These were exactly the kind of products or services that people may have heard of in an off-chance and wondered what happened to the wonderful idea.

"It should have grown, it had a lot of potential..." Manav sat next to the dog under the streetlamp, handing over some biscuits.

It was precisely to address this problem of loss, of invisibility, and access of small-scale businesses that Manav had decided to base his idea on the model of building a platform to allow these rising enterprises to gain an audience with potential donors, partners, and customers. Manav was going to build an online subscription-based website curation platform that would allow rising entrepreneurs to gain digital access, make their ideas visible not only on a national but a global scale.

He would provide digital literacy, how to make a cost-effective online presence, build brand image, create a market value and user-base, all with the help of cheap and easy algorithms that would help to set up websites on certain pre-designed templates. Moreover, it couldn't have been better timed! Everyone was moving to the online space because of the compulsion of the epidemic, and the evolution from offline to online was happening at a pace that would have taken a long time under ordinary circumstances.

Of course, this was a very rough idea and at this stage, only a figment of his imagination. But Manav knew it had a lot of promise and enough scope in the market. And just as Ved had suggested, it was time to focus his attention on his requirements. First and foremost, he needed to understand the legalities and technicalities of setting up such a model in cyberspace. For this, he needed someone who had both the expertise and the experience to guide him about the next steps. He had just the man in mind for this.

It was the first day at the convention. Manav, Satrupa, and Dev had been working all night for the past few nights, preparing their pitch, and they had woken up to barely make it to find enough time to freshen up and log in to the URL for the convention.

Amidst the crowd and the chaos, multiple hubs of presentations and panels, Manav was pinged by a familiar face, someone he had been hoping to meet more than anything else. Matsya was one of the friendlier faces in the bank circle. And this meant something, because most of the people around were very work-centric.

Matsya was an auditor who had visited the bank branch of Vaikuntha quite frequently in the years that Manav had worked in the office. Contrary to his impressions, Manav had been very pleasantly surprised with the cordial, insightful, and logical interaction he had had with Matsya, so much so that he had actively sought to speak to him, accompany him during his audit visits, and even exchange conversations outside of the workspace.

He had taken Matsya over to the little river that flows a little outside of his town when the senior auditor had to stay over the weekend for the year-end audit. They had sat together near the riverbank, enjoyed fritters with tea, and talked about all the adventures of the world. Of course, in their language, adventures meant business opportunities and observations. But that was a mystery they would only keep to themselves. Matsya had been very impressed with Manav's observation skills and passion and had offered his 'humble counsel' should Manav finally decide to pick up his dreams and convert them into reality.

And now, the time had come when Manav was ready to take him up on the offer.

Many years ago, when Matsya and Manav had met for the first time and were discussing business ideas while gazing at the stars above, Matsya had given what seemed like rather exhausting and time-consuming advice. "Manav, if you are determined to work on a product that helps small-scale businesses and helps you come up with a profitable business model, you will have to collect samples of each business type that you encounter during your life. You would meet them to sanction a loan, they could be some business you transact with personally, a neighbour, a friend."

Matsya had explained that it was this meticulous observation of what happened with the businesses and tracking of their success or failure that would lead to an in-depth understanding of the market, its trends, and its users, too. It was this advice, all those years ago, that had led Manav to keep a close watch. It was finally time to meet his mentor and discuss the next steps.

"I can't believe I am seeing you out of that shell, even though it's virtual, Manav!" Matsya teased him the moment they met in a private chat room, during a break! He had always encouraged Manav to sail out of that confined town, which, he claimed, was no match for the aspiring entrepreneur. But Manav decided that if at all it had to happen, it would in its own accord, in its due time. Pushing formalities aside and realizing the delicacy of time constraints, Manav jumped straight to the point. "It's time to set sail, Matsya. I am planning on building a platform that would help all businesses to stay afloat in the time of crisis, to cross their hurdle of setting seed."

Matsya was not surprised. He had already observed Manav's interest as a philanthropic entrepreneur when he had offered help and company to Matsya on his first visit, when he was utterly bored and clueless about the small town. The duo discussed the online platform at great length, identifying the strengths and weaknesses of the model. "More importantly, what I want to know from you is the cyber legalities, and how this whole funding process would work, if I were to pitch to international capitalists," Manav explained to him how his idea had a more universal appeal and therefore, why he should pitch to bigger fish than applying to a small-time loan.

"Not only will this give you a much better idea about the larger sense of the business, but it will allow you to be assessed by some of the bigger players in the game, gain insight from their perspective, and evaluate the scope of growth," Matsya said. He also helped Manav understand how setting up an online business, with third-party transactions and virtual monitoring, will also require an entirely different set of compliances than offline economics. "It won't work without transparency and participation. If you do not have the bulk, this model will be good for your consumers, but not work in your favour."

Manav meticulously took notes, both mentally and physically, about whatever they discussed. "How do I go about preparing a deck for funding?" This question had been haunting Manav for a while now. He was used to the system of small loans from banks, but Venture Capitalists were a different ball game altogether.

"Use your story. The story of all the businesses that you have observed and worked with, the ones that you aspire to carry forward with you on your platform. Tell them about what potential lies at the bottom of these businesses and how their rise or fall is not their fault but of the demon of the circle of crisis that lies below them," Matsya advised Manav on letting his learning, his personal growth and development, and his passion become the story and the deck of his pitch. If he were out to address the lives of entrepreneurs, he would first have to humanise them and address their challenges as humans.

This was more insight than Manav had come hoping for. It was decided that they would keep in touch, and of course, Manav would build his plan of action, build his next set of questions, and get back to him. Raising seed funding would be required in the next couple of months, but before that, he would have to build a solid concept and some initial proof to begin with. There was an entire ocean of possibilities before him. And it was up to him to choose the direction in which he was headed.

After the conclusion of the convention, and to take a much-needed break away from the screen, Manav went for a walk up on the terrace to marinate in his thoughts. The next steps were going to be very clear. He dialled in Satrupa and Ved on a video call.

"Do you ever switch off?" Satrupa was complaining, exhausted from her work at the newspaper and all the additional work for Manav. Ved just laughed, knowing well enough that in Manav's world, there was no concept of time. Having become accustomed to off-the-charts brainstorming sessions at 3 in the morning, he simply yawned and advised Satrupa,

"Please get yourself a cup of coffee, Satrupa. Let's get this over with. I am sure there are a lot of fresh ideas in Manav's brain after the convention, and before he dies of bursting with excitement, we should discuss while the dough is soft and fresh."

They joked around for a bit and then got down to business.

"So, as per Matsya's advice, I am going to get down and start working on the deck for funding for seed. I have a fair idea of what will be required, and Matsya will be helping out with some demo interactions connecting us with some VCs who he thinks might be interested in a lot of the online space. The good thing is that Matsya gave me insider news that not many people have started working in this direction, and if we work fast enough, we will have the edge of being the first and being most insightful for the bottom-up model."

Satrupa had already started searching for whatever information she could gather on tech-related ventures coming into India. "The good thing about online space is that our location will not be a disadvantage, and if we work on building a team, we can get lots of people to work remotely for us during the lockdown," she said. She also mentioned that there was news for the new fiberXP: Brahmand. It was the fastest internet service growing in the country, venturing into B and C cities and towns.

"This will be huge! We have an opportunity and an environment that can promote many existing online businesses to move in this direction," Manav exclaimed.

But Ved was thinking a couple of steps into the future. "Not just that," he reminded, "this makes it so conducive for conventional businesses to find hope to move to the online spaces in small towns. We will have a much better ground to make our pitch now!"

The midnight call was worth every second of the waking discomfort. The trio was super pumped about the next steps. They said their goodbyes, promising and asking each other to get some rest, but neither of them slept, with ideas and hopes bustling in their heads, each one just as excited as the other to the whole arena of opportunities that had opened before them. With Matsya's guidance, backing, and approval, Manav knew he was headed in the right direction and all he had to do now was persevere and follow with a straight head on his shoulders.

Moral: Every small action is paramount to the culmination of insight and perspective that ultimately becomes the experience factor in the journey of an enterprise. Even before explicitly diving into building the model, it helps to take an insight from those who can provide an outsider's opinion. And for that, it is important to build relations, because they become the strongest assets in the long run.

Chapter 3

Facing Failures

"I was running a successful banking organization," Manav stated. "But then there are days when everything goes south, and it's difficult to sit through the whole relay of challenges, watching the clock tick, waiting for the day to get over somehow, anyhow! But it's equally important not to let this be the reason you are down."

This is exactly what was happening with the rising entrepreneur in the small town of Vaikuntha. Manav had been working nonstop on preparing an ideation of his website model. He planned to make a business consortium of a sort, bringing visibility for small-time businesses by offering them affordable and customizable website building.

After the first guidance Manav had received from Matsya, along with the help of Satrupa and Ved, he had managed to pull off a couple of successful funding pitches, based on the venture capitalists they were going for. They had divided their strategy into two forms.

One was for the kind of venture capitalists who went for hardcore numbers and economics of things and cared about the viability and scaling of the business they were going to help out with. The other set was capital investors who looked for a story and scouted the entrepreneurial possibilities for impact. These were the kinds who believed that the impact was unique and loud, scale and business would match up in one form or another.

The interesting advice that Manav was following from Matsya was that both of these perspectives were right and appropriate, and both allowed for an approach to success. "So we just have to use two different languages to pitch the same ideas." Ved understood the fundamentals and started his research accordingly.

Satrupa, on the other hand, with her impeccable skills with people and communication, was helping Manav reach out to talented resources who could help build a team. It would be utopian to say that either of Ved's and Satrupa's efforts to support their friend were going in a flawless direction. There were many mistakes, many struggles, and a lot of rejections flooding their pitches, sprinkled with a little good news here and there. The trio was hanging on to these little trinkets to make the best of their situations.

It was a huge relief that Satrupa was there with Manav all through this phase. Because as much as Manav loved his friend, Ved could be a little too critical and harsh on him sometimes. Although Manav did not hold it against him and never complained about his brutal honesty, it did bruise his ego every now and then. This is where Satrupa's unending patience and understanding came as a rock of support for the aspiring entrepreneur.

"I think what he meant, when he said that your approach for the pitch was lukewarm, was that you can afford to be a lot more confident and aggressive," Satrupa always acted as the mediator. Although she did not like to get in between the duo, because she thought best to let them handle it on their own, she was also caught up in her dilemma of dealing with how it affected her relationship with Manav.

"Can you, for once, just take my side and admit that Ved is being wrong and arrogant about it?" Manav was particularly frustrated on one of the occasions and just couldn't handle the train of rejections that had been following him. He knew, somewhere deep down, that Satrupa was only trying to pacify him, but he just didn't want to be pacified right now.

Everything seemed to be going awry, and he was struggling with his internal turmoil about whether or not it was all worth it and whether he was making the right decision. And amidst all that confusion, he was afraid that he would appear weak in front of Satrupa. After all, it was not like their relationship was old and ripe, and that they understood each other's quirks and twists.

Satrupa was also struggling with her patience in the whole scenario. She noticed that Manav had been losing his temper a lot in the last couple of weeks. She would talk to her mother about it. Although she knew that talking to Ved would be a lot more relevant, she knew that it would be professionally and ethically inappropriate and could put the poor guy in an uncomfortable spot between the couple.

When Manav was spewing unintended poison, Satrupa only took a deep breath and said, "Manav, I am going to hang up now and take a break. I will talk to you once you are calmer and once I have found my patience back." She did the best she could, trying not to offend him but also letting him know that this behaviour was not ok. She was aware that this was the frustration talking, but as someone who had a lot of expertise in the fundamentals of communication, she knew that there was a better way of handling this, and she would make sure it was done correctly.

Thus, struggling with his emotions and battling with his professional choices, Manav fought on. In the last couple of months, Manav had spoken to a collection of engineers and designers, pitching to them his idea and trying to get them on board with his 'start-up' idea. Despite their differences, Satrupa was gregariously helping him out in scouting the right set of people and helping him prepare a script for the situation of his idea that would require a lot of convincing for people to join the business. It was still at a conceptual stage, so, of course, it was not going to be easy to bring many people on board without validation, let alone funding.

"What irony is this!" Manav was being grumpy and had been complaining to Ved for the last couple of days. "I can't raise funds till I have a validation, and I cannot get people for validation till I have some funds." Of course, it was a classic catch-22; Manav had seen all of this drama play out before him when he was on the other side of business. People would come to him for loan approvals with ideas, and it would be very difficult to validate their case based only on the concept.

"That's the cost of breaking the trend. For established ideas, there are smaller risks and hence people feel safe in betting on such path followers." Ved said. He was only reinstating what had been established year after year. "What you are doing has no head or tail, no precedence, and hence appears to be a big risk." Manav was nodding, while deep in thought about a way out.

"So basically, it is not the business idea they are uncomfortable with, but the risks of the unknown," Manav picked up from Ved's statement. "So, if I can bring them a sense of comfort, a proof of agreement from the target audience, and their willingness to buy this product, if it is available, that may work as a way to ease their anxiety about its success."

Brainstorming sessions helped Manav feel a little more comfortable about his pursuit. And right now, he was just so relieved that he had the option of choosing between Ved and Satrupa to switch between opinions, moods, and conversations. He was under so much stress that he feared he might lose himself in the pursuit of this mission, which had come to mean a lot more than just a business idea for him.

It is for this very mission, about being able to build a case for his potential customers, that Manav was trying to reach out to as many people as he could dig in his network, to churn some contribution from them, either in terms of money, or their expertise to get people on board for his idea. "The more I look into this model, the more I realize how much software Engineering is paving the way for all future business ideas," Manav was mumbling more to himself than anyone else, in the little house that had not been visited in months.

Ved and Manav would often log in and turn on their voice call and continue with their work, chatting up once in a while to give each other the feeling that they were still hanging out together despite the pandemic. After a while, it had stopped feeling weird, and they had gotten rather comfortable with this system. Manav had no one else to talk to except for Ved and Satrupa, while the other two still had their office colleagues, meetings, and assignments to work on, thus making it a multi-tasking opportunity for them to continue in between breaks.

"If I were an engineer, I would not need anyone's help but would sit to write all the preliminary code myself." He was almost frustrated. But Ved put a calming smile on from across the screen, sending a smiling emoji, as always, being a source of sense that he was. "But you know the financial mechanism inside out. If you had become an engineer, you would not have come to know about these intricacies, right?" Ved did have a point.

But this was not going to help Manav in his urgent need for tech support. That's where he always hit a dead end. He had all the dynamics clear in his head. But I don't have the expertise to build it. After spending days refining his business model, he had finally decided to start talking to his target audience to see if he could get some of them on board with his idea to prepare a case.

Every day, when he would log on to all social media websites, personal, professional, global, or local platforms, Manav would scan for potential users, trying to see what he could churn out from the sea of possibilities that lay before him. He knew that if he had to metamorphose the traditional mentality of the older generation around him towards the new, online means of business, he was going to need the help of their trusted, next gen representatives, their children, colleagues, neighbours, or people in their everyday lives who they sought help from in their digital struggles.

But so far, he had only stumbled upon dead ends. He would prepare his pitch, redesign it based on experience and responses, try greed, lure in with a profit partnership, tick off emotional vocabulary, but all his attempts failed between the tug of war of his idea against people's comfort zone of their beliefs. "To do this, I will need to make a pull for them." Manav decided.

It was decided then, Manav was going to set up an online workshop for young, like-minded people on some skill-building exercise and use it as an excuse to interact with them about his potential business model. "Keep your eyes and ears open, Manav, for you never know even the least imagined people can help you in this tug-of-war with possibilities," Ved reminded him, again and again, as they researched on the content that could be exciting and engaging enough for the youngsters.

It was one of these days, when potential liaison was being scratched and tapped on almost everywhere, losing boundaries between what is personal and what is professional, when Manav was in a deep discussion with the guide of the fitness club he used to be a part of. Earlier, he would go to the gym and often work on his stamina and muscle building, which had been quite the trend.

The gym had been seeing a dip in footfall ever since the lockdown, and Manav saw this as an opportunity to interact with the man who owned the property. "Maybe an off-season discount could be a good way to attract attention. If you get them hooked long enough, they will bring in more people for the discount."

Manav's simple solution had been quite enlightening for the guy, who beamed with excitement to sit with his calculation. "But that's not all. This virus and its effects are here for a while, and I don't see it going away in a month or even 3 months." Manav had been studying the pattern in the countries that had been hit long before India, and he could see that public places like gyms would be hit a lot more than singular services for about a year, maybe more. "What I would recommend is for you to invest in a good online class set-up. I can give you some advice on that. Get a good screen and sound system, invest in an application, and get all your customers back to join you on live online classes. More importantly, offer them online guidance and one-on-one counselling."

He explained how, during the lockdown, because of a lack of movement, many people were falling off the chart of their health plan, and how something like this, with disciplined coaching, would be a welcome respite. "What's more, if it's online, then you're opening up your business for those who do not or cannot step out of their homes, even without the lockdown. So you're taking the gym home to them!" This was far more impressive an idea than the poor business owner could have hoped for. "Manav, my friend, you are so smart. Do let me know if there's anything I can help you with!" he said.

Manav made a mental note of this; every network would come in handy for sure. It was during this conversation that they were requested to be joined by another regular on the same call. "Manav, I hope you don't mind, you have met him in the gym a couple of times, I thought it would be good to catch up together. Manav recognised the name on the request entry box of the other guy at the gym, whom he had seen working out consistently since Manav had joined the gym. "Oh, that's Kurma. He is not all that great with his workout skills. But man, is he hardworking!"

Manav had been immensely moved by the pure consistency of the guy whom he remembered to have been struggling with his bench presses, barely making it through the existing weights. He would sometimes have to reduce the weight and take another round, but he wouldn't just give up. He hadn't been like this ever since he joined a few months ago. Initially, everyone would make fun of him because he is not the strongest-looking guy around.

But his persistence has taken everyone by a jolt of surprise, and he has earned respect from both old and new players in the game! There was a lot to learn from the seemingly unimpressive man who was trying to build his body. Skinny arms and legs, with an almost larger-than-proportional torso from which a head was jutting out like a tortoise. But Manav got the impression that Kurma would be able to teach him a lot more than most people had done with their high talks.

Without a second thought, Manav readily encouraged him to join the group call. Kurma switched on his video, and they could see that he was huffing and puffing with the weights he had set up in a corner of his room. He was instantly greeted with a welcoming smile. "Hello, do you guys mind if I continue while we talk? I am almost done here," Kurma beamed. All that perseverance and frustration and still, not a sliver on his forehead! Manav thought to himself, liking this guy more and more.

Kurma decided to come straight to the point. "I have, for a while, admired your sheer dedication. I have seen you a couple of times before, but never really had a chance to talk. And today, it is just a matter of luck that you happened to join the call just when we were talking." Manav wasn't sure whether he was sounding like a complete idiot or was intimidating the man, but another flashing smile from Kurma immediately put him at ease.

"Hey man, I am glad you invited me into the group call. It is crazy that I was thinking of lowering another weight from the bar, but your praise has motivated me to push it! I am sure you can imagine how frustrating it can be to work out alone," Manav said. The two men simply laughed innocently at how a simple introduction had put them at such ease. After a little small talk, Manav exchanged some workout tips with Kurma, asking him about his work. When he got to know the guy ran an online coaching, Manav immediately proposed to catch up again sometime and discuss work with each other.

Kurma seemed more than willing to engage, and they ended that rendezvous with an exchange of their contact numbers. As Manav quit the group chat, letting the other two catch up with their conversation, he felt a little motivated himself to do some pushups and revise some of his body weight workout routine. As anyone who knows what a good workout session can do to you, he felt slightly better, slightly more hopeful, and in a way, inspired to continue stumbling with his work in the hope that something or the other was bound to come out of his experiments.

The small town of Vaikuntha had only recently begun to get its first few internet options, and a whole new platform of the World Wide Web was opening up for access. Although most of the people went for the popular choice of watching videos or simply getting tremendously active on social media platforms, a select few curious minds had begun to check out the various possibilities of learning and experiences. This, in the last couple of years, has led to a digital revolution in the town.

Tailors had become designers with ideas from the internet, people were learning to play different instruments, and ordering a whole new variety of products online. Newspaper distribution had seen a sudden dip ever since online news had become a rage. Manav remembered how, before the pandemic struck their little town, he would often walk to work to see a set of elderly people sitting around the young postman who would be reading out news from his mobile phone.

Initially, he had felt that this digitalisation was going to spoil the health of the younger generation, who seemed to be glued to their screens. But with time, when early curiosity had settled down and people had begun to transmit a wide range of knowledge and experience with one another, Manav was forced to change his opinion about the coming times and decided to ride the way and explore what the internet had to offer.

It was here that he had found out about the fundraising platforms for businesses, about the popularity of e-commerce websites, and how access and ease were changing over the internet. And now, with the pandemic here to stay, he could already see casual familiarity for the online space increasing amongst people of all age groups and backgrounds since that was the only kind of access available to the outside world while still being safe.

"Ved, I think I might have hit something here with Kurma." Manav was discussing a few days after the encounter. "If he is as determined in his work as he is at working out, I am quite confident that his online network of classes should at least be able to give us some stepping stones to building a part of our model."

As it turns out, Manav was not very far away from the truth. Within a week of their first meeting, Manav had invited Kurma to review a new online delivery that had just started circulating its ads to doorsteps and on local cable channels. "These guys are really good. I especially love their different flavours of tea and bread." Manav had ordered at least 5 varieties of tea off the menu, sending a package of the same products to Kurma's residence as well. It was all a part of his pitch, and he knew that impressions helped to subconsciously drive one's direction of decision making.

While Kurma enjoyed flavour after flavour of the green, masala, Kesar, fruity, and jaggery style of tea, from his end of the call, sitting in front of his laptop as the two conversed online, Manav went on to explain about his work experience and learning in the bank over the years. "The one thing I have learned is that ideas fail as businesses, even before they get a chance, not because they are bad ideas, but simply because they have not had the opportunity and no one has had the vision to give them a fair fighting chance." He spoke intently. "Look at this restaurant, the one where you're drinking your tea now, for instance. I can bet no place in the entire Vaikuntha or even cities around here makes as good or as many teas as this place.

And yet, before everything crashed because of the lockdown, it did not get a place in the main market where most of the paying customers go."

Manav knew he had Kurma's attention. "These are the kinds of businesses that need to be highlighted and promoted. That is not just serving a transactional purpose, but also is deserving of being leaders in their segment."

Kurma was smart enough to understand that Manav was not simply making small talk and had some agenda behind it. The important bit was that he was interested. Reading his body language, cut to the chase with his opening pitch. "You have an online platform and you understand what that kind of visibility and access can mean to a business, especially for small-time businesses or entrepreneurs who are just starting. That's what I am working on."

Manav continued to explain his model of creating an affordable online platform for enterprises to project their ideas, advertise their products and services, and even avail funding opportunities. "The challenge I keep getting stuck on is to have someone who can help me build a proof of concept, at least some visualization of the idea. I need engineers for that. But I don't have the right kind of access or money."

Kurma understood this dichotomy only too well. He candidly narrated his story of having to grind endlessly when he had first started his coaching offline. "Small towns just do not have that kind of exposure to support revolutionary ideas, although I have to admit that they are fast to adopt when it has become a safe space."

Kurma had one simple piece of advice for the young entrepreneur whom he saw himself almost a decade ago. "No matter what happens, do not give up on your trials. With sincerity and categorical hard work, it's hard to miss the right option!" But Kurma was not offering just words. He also had a solution that could just work for Manav's needs. His coaching had collaborations with professors in different parts of the country, and a lot of the students were engineers in the making.

He said, "We can simply form a collaborative platform where they work on your project as a part of their live learning experience. You do not have to pay them anything, but we will have to make this a barter system. In return, you have to give them entrepreneurial lectures and insights, especially in terms of financial learning. They will value this because they may never acquire this from their academic performances..."

Just like that, Manav had found a way out of the very first boulder he had been stuck with for months. It was this issue that prevented him from even being able to start with his ideas. The next steps were simple. He would have to prepare a solid idea that he could explain to the students, figure out how much of it was possible, and then set deadlines.

The conversation continued for a while longer as the duo exchanged ideas for a lot longer, only until there was a power cut at Manav's little apartment, and his internet crashed.

I will put you in touch with Kaustubha, my director of outreach and networking. She will take it from there.

Manav had received a text from Kurma. He had been researching Kurma's organization and team for a while, and he knew the name when it popped up on the screen. Kaustubha was known for her business expansion skills and was popularly called the 'gem' of Kurma's business. She was also his partner (both professional and personal), and they were a power-packed couple who broke the conventional norm of marital roles, especially for a small town. Even as Manav was contemplating sending her a text, his phone buzzed on its own, and he received a message from Kaustubha just that moment!

Hey Manav, hope I don't sound too rushed, Kurma just told me about you, and I thought I would very quickly discuss with you the number of people you are looking for in different fields and what plan of action you have in mind.

Manav was amazed at the woman's efficiency and power. Unlike his conversation with Kurma, which gave a more visionary sense of ideas, Kaustubha seemed like the exact opposite, with specific, categorical, and crisp discussions.

Happy to touch base with you, Kaustubha. Give me a day, and I will get back to you with a concrete list of all that we require.

He texted back, a little embarrassed at his lack of preparedness. And yet, this short conversation had been very enlightening for him to understand what a prompt and persistent approach with categorical understanding meant like. He would have ideally mulled over the ideas for a few days, chewed on what message to send to the stranger, and how to start the conversation. And just like that, Kaustubha had popped out on her own.

He was quite impressed to see how the equation between the duo worked, and wondered about his equation with Satrupa. They did have a compatible connection, and they did look out for each other.

"Once people hear that my idea is not just floating in mid-air, I am very sure they would be open to listening more intently!" Manav was sipping his late-night tea while discussing with Ved, while Satrupa joined them on the call.

After a few months of contemplation and tight budgeting, he had given up his apartment and moved in with Ved to save on the rent. After all, he was going to need all the money he could save, especially since he had to quit his job. But he was hopeful this was going to work out all right.

In the daytime, Manav worked on all the ideas and models. In the evening, he contacted potential clients and funders, both online and offline, and at night, he prepared for his lectures with the students, worked on the blueprints of the platform, and brainstormed with whoever felt appropriate. He spent a generous amount of time, while on calls or in discussions, helping out Ved with all his household chores, in his humble way of thanking his friend for giving him a roof and a bed.

Satrupa, on the other hand, would help by sending in files and connecting them for any media advice and contacts, not just in Vaikunth but everywhere else. On the condition that the three of them met only under safe circumstances, with social distancing, the three had also hung out at Ved's terrace.

Although Satrupa and Manav had met hundreds of times before, their equation had changed in the last few months, and before now, they had only been talking on the phone or online. Things were changing now. They were getting to see each other in person, even though it was six feet apart, behind masks.

But it was a wonderful feeling and a wonderful time to be together. Not just because of the new phase of their relationship, but also because of the professional journey they were all embarking on together, which pushed their potential, interests, and creativity. To have Ved with them, with complete dedication and insight, was what made every moment of burning the midnight oil worth it. Of course, these moments of gratitude and camaraderie will never be forgotten and prove way more valuable than any high-sounding positions in the world!

But while he was getting the work done, was he getting the right feeling? Was he not losing the plot? Was he moving away from the original intent? The questions would have to wait. He had an organization to build.

Moral: Most successful entrepreneurs, while beginning with humble origins, did not shy away from putting themselves out there and kept their eyes, ears, and minds open to learning. Despite all the expertise or knowledge you may have, as an entrepreneur, it helps to continue the growth curve.

Chapter 4

The Power is in Your Mind

They say that the world is an ocean of opportunities, and if you are headed in the right direction, consistently diving into the depths, you are bound to find the pearls. But determination is not the only quality that will get you deeper and richer, so to speak, in your endeavours.

Being confident and assertive plays a very important role in the life of a leader, and these are attributes that we sometimes either ignore or underestimate the impact of. But for every mistake made and every challenge faced, there is a lesson to be learned. This is all that Manav could think of, drenched in sweat, pounding the streets in his shorts and a hoodie against the biting wind.

It was 2 degrees, and at that time when even stray dogs were reluctant to venture out. He could only get out late at night when there was absolutely nobody on the road, and it was safe from any infection. With all the warmth and good cheer that the day's work had brought, the temperature now seemed more excruciating. What added more was that he felt like he had no choice.

How did this affect Manav? His clients were getting desperate. If there was one thing he had picked up from Indian patterns, it was the fact that seasons and festivals play a tremendous role in the user patterns of clients, customers, and everyone with money or looking for money. It had been the same in all the years. Even more so this year because of the lockdown. Although the initial complete shutdown was lifting in bits and pieces now, overall travel, production, and purchases had all been affected.

All through the monsoon, the buying season had been rather dull. There were no festivals, and almost all outdoor activities, events, and celebrations stopped until the ambiance was better, while the market struggled to keep afloat. But with the onset of winter begins the first flights of purchases, accounts, and contracts that continue till the next financial year. With this in mind, he had been working for the last few months endlessly and diligently, with the collaboration of several online resources, and he had managed to get together with his networking and the networking of others.

Kurma's contacts and network had brought him a lot of opportunities. In the last month or so, he had diligently planned his curriculum to deliver his end of the deal of providing insight and lessons on financial understanding. And he was getting the better end of the deal. His online platform for collaboration, fundraising, and website building had already undergone its beta testing, and the results had been quite satisfying.

Many small business owners, whom he had reached out to individually, had been attracted to the idea, especially because it came with an easy subscription model that did not go very heavy on the pocket.

The second good thing working in their favour was that Manav's team had been providing a lot of tech support as a part of their customer retention and support mechanism. This was great for new business starters because they had one less hassle to worry about.

The beta phase also saw several old businesses getting curious about this online version of their enterprises because of the support.

"All these years, I had heard so many people say we should convert online, but we neither have the expertise nor any information about how to even begin this process," a restaurant owner from Odisha had told Manav's research intern in a survey call.

The restaurant owner had initiated a process of setting up an online order platform through them and had reported a 65% increase in his business!

Many such initial proofs of concept had brought Manav and his now-growing team to start functioning in a bigger and more structured format. Especially in these times, when online had become the new trend and everyone was following suit, it made things easier and more convenient, both in terms of how easy it was to show customers success stories and also how much more conducive the environment was getting to the online approach of all levels of business and transaction.

"One of the first things we should do is to start marketing our product more widely so that there's enough revenue flowing in," Ved had expressed. He had been taking more and more initiatives and ownership and had transformed with time from just being someone whom Manav could bounce ideas off to look after the operations of the rising e-commerce platform.

"I think, before anything else, we should at least come up with a name for our business! Right now, it's a whole statement to explain who we are and what we do," Satrupa chipped in. Most discussions had converted from being random brainstorming during dinner or a walk to online meetings with other team members.

Manav now had a set of engineers connected with him, some interns for sales calls who also doubled up as research and development guys. They had just recently officially hired Satrupa to help them with brand building and management. By hiring, it meant that Satrupa was working for them after work hours and on weekends and would be paid as soon as the initial revenue targets were met.

That was probably the equation for almost all team members who had come on board. For now, things had worked out ok, but soon, they would need to start paying people and hiring better people, if things went the way they were going right now.

Manav had been mulling over this whole question about a name and a brand for the business for quite some time now. Most businesses he had seen offline were named so randomly that they had no depth. Online businesses, on the other hand, had shown a trend that would not match his target audience, who were new or small business owners.

"It has to be something that reveals the opportunity we are bringing for them. It is like giving them a new look, a new set of powers that they can use," Satrupa said. She had been taking a more active and hands-on involvement with the business rather than being some sort of advisor in the background. Satrupa was spot on with her diagnosis of the brand image. Everyone on the video call was nodding their heads.

After a few more such sessions and exercises that she had held with the team and some consumers, both existing and potential, Satrupa had come up with a name that was voted in favour of unanimously. "We'll call it 'Avatar'. In the digital world, it is a common terminology reflecting what form or profile you pick for your activities. In the traditional sense, it has a larger-than-life impression of an appearance with a feeling of godliness, something that is both aspired to and revered."

Her pitch had been perfect, and the many expressions of the team as they played around with the word in their head made Manav know for sure that Avatar was the right choice. The more Manav worked hands-on with Satrupa, the more he was in awe of her intelligence.

What he felt worked most in their favour was how intimately their thoughts matched with one another. Since they both knew how the other would think, it was rather easy for them to understand the logic, the endorsements, and even the disagreements!

Ved did have his concerns about bringing Satrupa onboard officially, strictly for professional purposes, but Manav comforted him, "I know what you mean. I understand the sentiment, many people shy away from mixing business life with personal matters."

Manav respected his friend's opinion and approval more than anything else. He wanted to make sure there was no air of discomfort around. He added, "But there are so many traditional businesses that are run within the family, right? And isn't this a great chance to practice and grow as professionals? Besides, you have said so yourself that you are blown away by her speed and accuracy at understanding the needs of the market and translating into a language of communication."

Manav spoke honestly, completely aware of how risky this could be, both for professional and personal compatibility. He knew that now and then, the couple got into a tiff. It was almost always involving their differences, however, just about how they differed in an opinion about something, or had a different perspective. Most of all, their difference was about their response to situations. Of course, this was disturbing for both of them from time to time.

"Well, you shouldn't have snapped at the customer care representative. He was only doing his job!" Satrupa would tell him to observe the way he would behave with other people. Manav knew her intention was honest and sincere. That was just the way she thought.

But Manav also had to steer away from admitting his own mistakes each time. He insisted, "The situation was not that black and white. You know how exhausted I was, and I have reported the issue of spam calling multiple times, but they do not respond!"

However, the tiffs were more or less harmless, except for leaving moments of space and silence between the couple. Which was good in the way that it allowed them to clear their thoughts and reflect on each other's opinions. The good thing was that their professional compatibility allowed them to sync in with each other on all matters, more often showing each other how the other person's opinion would change them for the better.

"There's this one thing that matters more than the little differences of opinion is that our judgment clicks," Manav told Ved, almost clarifying and endorsing the decision to bring Satrupa on board. Do you see how I nodded immediately after the last interview call for the business lead? She was thinking exactly on the same lines." Manav observed the little things. And he was always glad to see that Satrupa did too. Instead of falling for the larger appearance and fancy words, they would look out for signals and subconscious expressions.

It was getting more and more obvious to him every day why he liked Satrupa and she liked him, and why they would be good together in the long run.

With Avatar having gone live, several queries were coming in about the business. Satrupa was leading the march on many fronts at this critical hour. She said, "Instead of direct advertising, you should approach indirect, testimonial-type, word-of-mouth. That is very specific to the target audience you are catering to."

A set of interns was immediately tasked to advertise setting off discounts for all feedback and testimonials given. Of course, this, coupled with a good set of customer treatment, got many clients to give genuine, positive feedback. It did not take long for Avatar to start appearing as a recommended brand for small-town businesses in and around Vaikuntha to convert their businesses online or to enable e-commerce services.

"Avatar will make your business go beyond the limits of your shop and help you find a customer base in different parts of the country..." someone said.

"Avatar made it easy for my clients to reach me and order from the comfort of their home," said a small-town painter."

"I managed to raise 10 lacs to start my business with the help of the advertisement-based subscription that Avatar offered me," a happy studio owner claimed.

"In these difficult times, any hopes I had for a flourishing business had been curbed because of the lockdown. I was already wondering how I was going to repay the massive loan I had taken to build the outlet. But looks like this online conversion will save me some face, and, help me save some money too, considering that a lot of capital and operations costs will go down," another business professional piped.

Multiple opinions and feedback were coming in, and it was an opportune moment to broadcast the relevance in all ways possible. Manav was trying hard and fast to spread the word and was inviting as many queries and trials as possible. It was here that Manav was forced to suddenly halt his operations and open his eyes wide at his mistake.

When a random query came in, Manav's team virtually lay their heads at the feet of their potential client, telling them not only about the product and its benefits but everything about the team, the core of the business model, and sometimes, even offered to show them some accounts to demonstrate how systems worked. And that was all fine until it was not!

One particularly insistent client had been pushing hard to understand the backend mechanism of Avatar and was persistent in being told every detail about the business model. "I can't invest until I know what the root of your business is," he said. He had claimed to the sales team. He had been so bullish with his approach that, after a point, the juniors were forced to bring in Ved to handle the potential giant of a client. "We couldn't afford to anger him and didn't know how to say no to his demands."

They were helpless indeed. It was after having understood most of the business model that Hiranya suddenly went silent and stopped enquiring about Avatar. They tried to reach him a few times, to check if he was still interested, but Hiranya seemed to be giving them a cold shoulder. It wasn't until a couple of months later that Manav realized the hard truth.

Hiranya had been sleuthing away into the business ever since he had read some reviews and after digging as much as he could, he had started to develop a copy of Avatar, advertising it almost along the same lines, using the same brand colours to create a sense of confusion in the market, thereby causing a split in the customer base. It was alarming because there were several clients, albeit a small one, who had even begun exploring what the competition was offering.

Once this information was revealed, Manav felt like he had been shoved into the deepest trench of an ocean! "How can people be so blatantly fraudulent?" He was flabbergasted. This could not only cause a lot of damage in terms of business but would also ruin their brand value.

Manav was visibly shaken by this discovery, and he couldn't stop himself from going online again and again to see the advertisements being posted by Hiranya. His social media was fast flooding with this 'unique business idea' he had and how he was going to change the way small businesses viewed and functioned with e-commerce. Even though Hiranya did not have his product ready to go, he had already started selling the idea at a frighteningly fast pace and louder volume.

Manav was completely submerged in these thoughts while coming back from his run early one morning. Generally, after the run, he did some warm-ups and stretches and used that time to listen to the latest news and developments from around the world after slowing down and picking up fresh fruits from the local suppliers. He had been trying to do that to keep as many vendors sustained and in business during the lockdown, since a lot of their purchases had come to an unfortunate stop.

Manav wasn't keeping his eyes open during the last leg of stretching, and with earphones plugged in, he didn't even hear the call to 'watch out' from a bicycler behind him, spilling his bag of morning supplies around the pavement. "I am so sorry!" Manav exclaimed automatically, first instinctively replacing the mask on his face from around his neck and immediately bending down to pick up the packets of spices scattered across. When he saw the feet of the man opposite him standing stubbornly on the ground, he was forced to look up. When he saw who the man was, he raised his eyebrows in surprise.

"Varaha! What are you doing back in Vaikuntha?" He jumped up, wanting to hush the man, but remembered just in time about social distancing. He replaced it with a warm salute, a signature salutation some of the old gang used to exchange many years ago. "It's been what, 3 years?" The man in front of Manav gave out a hearty laugh, returning his hug in just as much of a comic style as from several years ago.

Varaha had left his bank job a few years ago and moved to another city, 'to make something better out of his life instead of listening to a boss who doesn't know even as much as our peon', as he claimed. Varaha was rather straightforward and quite assertive in his demeanour.

Anyone who met Varaha always left with quite an impression of his strong personality. Not only was he extremely full of confidence, but he was always very categorical about what was ok and what was not ok for him. There was no scope for nonsense in his life.

"Why the hell did you just apologize to me, you idiot? I am the one who was busy texting while walking!" That was classic Varaha right there! Manav had gotten along really well with him in the past, more because he was quite focused on getting better in life and did not humour any nonsense. It just struck him that Varaha could teach him quite a lot.

"You're coming for breakfast with me. We have a lot to discuss," Manav insisted. Varaha recognized and respected that look of determination vehemently and followed without any further questions. "Let me adjust some pending tasks while you collect your groceries..." Varaha also told him to expect company and left with a smile.

Within the next hour, Manav was joined by Varaha and a woman who looked like she was very flustered about something.

"Manav, please meet my wife, Bhudevi." Manav had known from the smile that Varaha would introduce him to a partner. He was curious to see whether it would be the same woman he had been dating all those years ago. And he was very happy to see that he was and had ended up marrying her.

After the pleasantries had been exchanged, Manav quickly briefed his ex-colleague all about Avatar, especially about the part where Hiranya was trying to usurp his idea and popularise it as his. "I don't want to discourage you, Manav, but I don't think I am surprised. The guy who couldn't stand up to a stranger who spilled his bag can't have stood his ground to a more than necessary nudging from a 'potential customer'."

Varaha was carefully sorting out the green chilies from his plate, putting them aside on a napkin. "I am sure you were not assertive enough even when he asked you about your business model. You were so busy trying to keep him happy that you didn't even realize you were being a doormat!" This was too close to reality for Manav's comfort. He had only now realized that instead of blaming Hiranya was being a prick, he had to take responsibility for what was going on.

Up until now, Bhudevi was a curious listener, but now, it was her turn to speak up. "You're running a business. That, too, is a smart one. Your idea is good, and by the way you describe the reviews and businesses using your platform, I can tell that the product is worth something. You are going to have to act like an owner now."

Manav was surprised to hear such assertiveness from the woman he had only gotten to know an hour ago. But the more she spoke to him, the more he understood that she was just an equal in Varaha's business and was carrying the bigger burden of responsibilities in the internal affairs of their enterprise.

It seemed like a healthy partnership that the two had developed, but it did seem to Manav that there was a lot of power play at work that the words would express. It was amazing how these little sub-texts kept rolling in his mind these days, especially when he met a couple and would always equate other people's relationships with his relationship with Satrupa.

All of this was twirling in the back of his mind as Bhudevi narrated her own experiences from her early professional stage. "I was rather benign and giving, early in my career, Manav. This is why I have learned the hard way how competitors and consumers can sometimes be ridiculously exploitative."

She talked about how she had started her own independent business of housing facilities, but was driven to the level of exhaustion of her resources because of some bad and naive decisions made in good faith. "Only then did I learn that being assertive, and sometimes aggressive, is what the market needs from you as an entrepreneur," Bhudevi said.

She confessed that although she had been doing excellent work on the ground, her skills in the online and e-commerce domain had not been strong enough to save her from plagiarism and aggressive hackers. "Had it not been for Varaha, I would have simply been crushed like a gullible target in the online space."

Varaha continued to explain how clients and customers tend to value those people less who crumble easily and are way too eager to mould themselves, their services, and value for the demand of the client. "You have to set a benchmark for yourself, evaluate your potential, and then set it in stone."

He also went on to talk about how such 'curious clients' always come in with bait and try to dig as much as they can. Just as Varaha had begun giving Manav hell for being so gullible, he got a call from a number that showed up as Hiranya's. Seeing

Manav nervous, Varaha glared into his eyes and spoke sternly. "Now, you will not run away from this. Pick up the call, let him say whatever he wants to, and then give him a clear and solid piece of your mind. Make sure there is no mincing of words."

Manav reluctantly picked up the phone, where he heard a very polished, almost snaky voice of Hiranya who was apologizing about the radio silence in the last few weeks, and asked if they could quickly figure out a deal for him so he could sign the contract the next day. "But, before I do that, I just need a list of some of your clients. You know, for some reference work, and to get some background confirmation. Nothing against you, Manav, but I am sure you understand business."

Bhudevi, who had been listening on speaker phone, along with the other two, tilted her head up, as if in complete rejection of the sly usurper. That gesture was enough for Manav to understand what he had to do. He took a deep breath in, let go of the spoon on his plate that he had been fiddling with for the last few minutes, and spoke, "Mr. Hiranya, I am so glad you are interested in partnering up with us for your needs. I assure you, the testimonials that our website speaks of, and the data we shared with you in the past, are all genuine. Besides, we design custom-made solutions for each client. If you are not happy with the pitch we have made for you, I doubt there's much else to convince you." Manav couldn't believe he was saying these things. He had never been so direct in his life!

Within the week, Manav sent out a legal notice to Hiranya's company, requesting them to take down data shared by them in their advertisements and for theft of intellectual property. Hiranya could think that he was bluffing, but that was hardly a chance he would be able to take, caught by such surprise he was!

Hiranya dropped most of the content he had been posting after being explained in great detail about the legal implications if Manav took him to court. Manav, on the other hand, learned not to underplay his position and work on conveying the merits of Avatar just as sincerely as he was committed to fine-tuning the portal for new businesses to start registering.

With the help of Satrupa and Ved, the team started coming up with simple but effective social media content to start creating a strong buzz for Avatar. "Remember, people. Your age or the number of years will not define the way you will be treated by anyone in life. It is your clarity and confidence and the content of your knowledge that should govern the steps you take. Let us work hand in hand and in the same way we help our partners realize their worth, we make sure that our partners know our worth too!"

Manav left his team of youngsters with a pearl of wisdom he had picked up recently. It was time to go for another dive!

Moral - Early entrepreneurs often struggle with a sense of accomplishment and identity. This not only makes them doubt their capacity but also makes the world judge them with a bullish attitude. Make a product to the best of your ability, and if you believe it is rich, then defend it with all you have, and if you do not respect your product, nobody else will. In the space of e-commerce, especially for conventional businesses, the competition is tough, and players are experimenting hard and fast. In such a scenario, not only is it important to keep quality at its peak, but it is equally important to keep your brand a part of the leading conversation. Advertising and marketing your product and its achievements are just as important, if not more important than, the product itself. And if it is not done

in time, there is a high risk of losing a significant market share. Just because you were the market pioneer doesn't mean you will be the leader, unless you fight to keep that position intact.

Chapter 5

The Price of Overcommitting

You know that feeling when things are looking good, right? There are no traffic jams. The radio is playing just the right kind of music. The shower runs at just the right temperature of water. All clients are listening to you, and you are on a creative roll! That is the kind of feeling that lifts you in the air and makes you believe that you can fly. And even though that may be the best feeling in the world, that is precisely the feeling you should be extremely wary of, in all aspects of life, but even more so when there is a lot at stake. Otherwise, it does not take long to lose sight of the ground and fall flat into the pile of mess you may have created for yourself. Now, that may or may not have been exactly what was going on with Manav. There's no need to get ahead of ourselves.

But it would be fair to say that Avatar had kicked off well, and with the humble but efficient team that Manav had managed to put together with the help of his friends and networking, he had managed to build up a solid array of clientele for the web portal of Avatar. It had not even been a month since Manav had run into his old friend Varaha and his wife Bhudevi.

At that time, Manav had been in quite a vulnerable position and had been struggling to rid of a usurper who had been trying to ape his idea and get a hold of his clients by pretending to be a client who could potentially bring him a lot of business for himself and also for the people who he had a lot of influence over in his network.

However, Varaha and Bhudevi had taught him a valuable lesson about not falling for the trap of people taking advantage of his business. He had learned to be assertive and authoritative and managed to get rid of all the plagiarism that his business was plagued with. Another valuable lesson that Manav had been implementing since was letting all clients, associates, and even colleagues know the true value of Avatar, never underestimating themselves during the pitch, something he had picked up from Bhudevi. Thus, Manav found himself in a very comfortable and confident position right now.

The e-commerce platform had picked up quite a few subscriptions in the last few months and even made it to the banner coverage on a tech news online paper.

Not only is this a unique format of e-commerce, but with Avatar, Manav, the founder and CEO, has also intelligently brought to life a platform that would bring business visibility, opportunity, and possibility of funding and growth to entrepreneurs who would probably not stand a chance without any seed funding.

The article had done so much PR that Manav had had to appoint a couple of sales representatives just to cater to the inbound calls and inquiries.

"This is just the kind of break we needed! We have nothing stopping us anymore. Our name has been published, our credibility has been established, and we now have a completely open, untapped market to dig into, waiting at our disposal with all the success stories and client base to speak for us." He was speaking fast and quite candidly on the video call. Manav's excitement had crossed all boundaries. He had rampantly expanded his sales team so they could reach out to an even larger customer base while the iron was hot.

"So far, we have been pushing for a small-entrepreneur base to join in for our basic model of subscription, with just basic adjustments of the algorithm." Manav was talking to his Sales and Marketing team about the newly purchased online platform for virtual meetings and conferences. It had come rather expensive, but he believed that this was just an investment they would make, and the returns would follow easily.

"We have to think about the future, people. This pandemic doesn't look like it is about to go away anytime soon, especially not completely. So even if we turn to office space later, we will still have a platform to connect with a larger platform online and to hold conferences at a much lower cost."

Manav had a very valid point because even when the pandemic subsided, the new normal of interaction and business would become quite different from what it used to be before the virus spread around the world. The online space was here to stay.

Pumped with a lot of enthusiasm with the rising numbers, Manav flashed a big smile from across the big screen, "It's time to take it to the next level. We have to work with a new set of audiences now. These are people who are not just looking for an online platform but their customized idea of execution, people who want a more efficient system to handle bigger projects of e-commerce, display of live projects, and interactive interfaces. We will build it all!" Manav completed his brief for a more aggressive strategy with his team and left to take an interview.

"We are working on getting an advertising agency on board that can help us cover more solid ground and represent our success and service to a wider audience," Satrupa said.

She had been working tirelessly with the advertising front, keeping up with the hasty demands of Manav. She could not necessarily agree with his approach, but he had a mission in mind, and she was not going to stop him from pursuing it.

Her understanding of the advertising space of online business was still evolving, and Satrupa was not going to let any ego get in the way of admitting her need for getting help in the matter.

She had told Manav that she was going to pursue the next steps and get a brief on the next steps. He smiled and waved everyone goodbye before logging off, imagining a whole set of chaos, excitement, and craziness to take over the group call, full of people who had just been shown the face of a very promising future.

There's a thing about humble people from small towns; they think things more thoroughly and intently than most. The reason? They have a low risk-taking position and capacity, and therefore, every step taken is questioned a thousand times. This may sound like a growth-crippling drawback to many, but when you look closer, it is one of the best perspectives to come on board in a start-up, to make sure that there's scrutiny at every angle.

When Manav left the conference meeting, he had expected actions jumping into motions, browsers flying, and people brainstorming and throwing ideas as they do in slow motion in a film with a scene of a high-tech firm. That was not the case here. There was a long moment of silence because both sales and marketing were people whom he had brought on board from in and around Vaikuntha. The simple, critical people who scanned the ground a thousand times before stepping on it.

"What is he talking about? How are we going to move on to a new segment altogether when we still have work to do on the existing product and market?" Satrupa, who had been heading marketing for a while and understood the sentiment of the team, who was already working very hard, now spoke when no one else was ready to address the elephant in the room.

"I know this sounds very strange to all of us, and this will mess up a lot of planning and targeting. But we have to understand where Manav is coming from. He has targets in his plans, and although it may not be clear at this stage, he has plans to expand our operations too," Satrupa said.

She had to tread carefully to make sure that she did not come across like she were biased towards her partner and covering his tracks. She did not want to be perceived to be representing the other side of the management because then she would never be able to work as closely with her colleagues as she could right now, being candid and pally, pushing them and tugging them as though she were one of them.

Satrupa understood and appreciated what a critical position and role she enjoyed in Avatar, and she had to work twice as hard to make sure that she was taken seriously and not have her participation interpreted as a luxury she had stolen because of her relationship with Manav. They had decided to be open about their relationship within the organisation, as a clear indication of transparency and good faith. But it was neither an easy decision to make nor to follow. In a sticky situation like this, Satrupa had a clear strategy. It was a strategy that Manav had also learnt from her now and used just as sincerely.

Satrupa never went against or criticised Manav's point of view in public. She would put across her point as any teammate would, and she would also make sure that even behind his back, she held up the opinion, even if she could have personally disagreed with it. It was only when they were alone or with Ved that any differences of opinion were discussed. Manav did the same in turn.

Another thing they had done to keep all edges smooth was to make sure that Ved, Manav, and Satrupa always discussed major decisions or announcements amongst themselves first before announcing them to the teams. So this time, too, when there was discomfort, Satrupa did not make it obvious and tried to even the odds with her team.

There was a mixed set of opinions about this, and after much brooding, the consensus was that the boss must be right and that Manav must have thought of these things and had a bigger plan in mind.

The team, with complete faith in their leader, set off working with double strength and numbers to bring on board even more clients. The epicentre of Avatar, which was Ved's spare room one floor above his house, which was located almost in the middle of the marketplace, looked directly down to the window of the gym in the opposite building, and one could see all sorts of people working out in all sorts of manner.

However, during the lockdown, just as everything else had shut down, so had the gym. But Manav had been a frequent visitor there before and now felt only obliged to help the business out. He was the one who had suggested the gym owner set up an online course for people to exercise under guidance with body weight routines.

While on call, Ved, Satrupa, and Manav would often go and stand against the glass windows and watch professional bodybuilders, enthusiasts, wannabes, and fitness freaks, all working out on screens from their respective locations at different paces, with different tools. It was an interesting reflection, not very different from what Avatar was also trying to do with the aspirations of rising entrepreneurs. It was a constant contest between things they were trying to achieve against what they could achieve.

"It's crazy, but there's always lessons and inspiration around, wherever you want to see, if only you look with the right eyes," Ved and Satrupa were discussing, while Manav was stuck in a business brief with wonder. With their sales chart increasing constantly, Ved had sent out a group notification to inform the team that just within a fortnight of their strategy shift, they had bagged a large project from an e-commerce site that was converting the business model of a very prominent and prestigious company to the online mode. It seemed that Manav had been right all along. They were already setting foot on the larger boats now, and it wasn't long before they would be in the league of the big players.

"I just got off a call with Vamana, the Head of Operations at Universe, one of our newest clients. He has asked us to show him a demo in three weeks. I am sure we'll be able to deliver. Right, team?" Manav was more imposing than asking on the sync-up call that evening.

He had met Vamana over a video call and had swarmed him with a whole ocean of confidence. "Mr. Manav, we are looking for a steady and secure site where our bidding for construction can happen with a seamless experience. In all these years, we have been functioning offline, and I have realized that increasing timely access and live experience of projects is the new norm. Do you think you will be able to provide us with that on our website?"

Vamana had spoken quite directly and simplistically with Manav, showing that he knew exactly what he wanted, and despite his mammoth reputation, there was no exhibition of pomp or show around him. "I am looking for a practical and effective solution, and I want it in a reasonable time. Do you think you can give me that?"

Manav did not think twice. "Let your team share the timelines, and I will deliver." It was as simple as that. On the way out of what Manav believed to be a very successful meeting, Manav was beaming at Ved. "You know what this means, right? We have set foot with the big players. The smaller fish will come in on their own now."

Ved was conspicuously quiet. "Do you think we will be able to deliver?" Manav just gave him a shrug, too happy to let any cynicism bring him down. "We will have to. We will work twice as hard, commit to the work, and I am sure we will be able to deliver."

Manav was not even realizing that he had already begun digging nails into his foot. While he had been pitching aggressively to the bigger clients, to keep the money flowing, he had also commanded the sales team to go all in with smaller clients to keep the money flowing. "No client is a small client," he had said to motivate them, when in reality, he had not been able to focus where Avatar's attention should be at this stage.

After his conversation with Vamana, Manav was desperate to prove to him and himself that the commitment was legitimate and he would be able to present the mock-up in three weeks. How was he going to achieve this? He had pushed the priorities around for some of the smaller clients, delaying their deliverables till Vamana's job was done.

"We're hiring more people. But till they get here and start helping you out, you have got to push yourself. This is a real opportunity to prove your competence under pressure!" Manav was talking to his design and tech team.

Now, you have to remember that Avatar was built not on the most solid foundation in terms of resources. Manav had scraped together people and tools through networking and a lot of liaising. Not many people on his team came with a lot of expertise and experience, but they were truly and deeply committed to making Avatar proud. This commitment had brought them this far, and in fact, impressed everyone in their working circles. It had been a mighty learning curve for them. But that does not take away the fact that these were, after all, people with not the best and in-depth experience. When push came to shove, with the massive increase in traffic on Avatar's portals, a lot of code began to break.

The design team found themselves at a crisis of either handling existing requests of clients, with their numbers increasing every week, or catering to the demands of building things from scratch for the giants. With the three-week deadline almost coming to an end, the team was at its shreds, working around the clock, often sleeping in the office. It was not like Manav was oblivious to this. He was spending most of his time connected with them, either working with them or talking to clients, trying to pacify or push their demands.

"We can do this, guys. We can pull it all together. Once this is over, you can all take a long break, and a lavish dinner on me!" Manav was constantly motivating his team. He believed that just enough push would help them all achieve all the targets. What he was not realising was that there was a threshold to capacities, both human and technological. And if he was not careful, he would break one or another.

At the end of the three weeks, Manav and Ved logged in to connect from the posh but simple office of Manav, which had been set up in the second-floor room. With the backend team working with them online to present the demo, Manav walked up in front of the projector to show Vamana and his team what they had brought to the table.

As his presentation started, a stoic-looking woman who was very diligently looking at her notes from what looked like a pile of notebooks seemed to take on the lead, and everybody else sat back on cue. Later, Manav would get to know her well as Kirti; she was the co-founder, with Vamana was the COO. She was the one who took all major decisions, this was clear to Manav within the next few minutes from even across the multiple screens in the meeting.

While he was still evaluating his situation, Kirti shot a question that took Manav by surprise. "Where are you planning on hosting our website? From what I understand, this alone will take up a huge chunk of your cloud space."

While Manav was still struggling to assure him that arrangements were being made, Kirti took the second step of interrogation. "What level of cybersecurity is arranged for our transactions? If there's a common algorithm pattern for all businesses on your portal, then aren't we vulnerable to every single breach?"

Manav had not thought this through. Forget about not having the right answer, he suddenly realised that he did not, most probably, have even the capacity to deal with this level of security right now." But this was not all. When the final step came and it was time to present the demo, something broke, a backend design, and completely disrupted the user interface. There was complete havoc in the tech room with the tech team.

We didn't get a chance to dry run the last part!

Someone had texted Manav. He didn't know what to say. He had only just realised what a bad ditch he had gotten himself into. He looked at Vamana, who had a very straight and neutral expression on his face, very different from the person he had seen in their first call. This was a person who had shown his full power without even saying a word and shown that he could not and would not be taken lightly.

Manav crashed into the chair, with a feeling that Vamana had walked all over him. It was only that he realised that he had wrung his well too dry. With the teams being stretched to their edge, their confidence, attention and capacity had all thinned out, not just because they were, for the first time in their career, dealing with such a prestigious client, but also because there were too many other active users for Avatar algorithm and something or the other had kept breaking or getting stuck simultaneously and the designers, coders, marketing team, sales team, they had all been way over their heads in this one.

Manav's motivation and constant push had kept them excited and pumped up enough to keep going, but motivation alone is not fuel enough when there's no expertise or substance to build work on!

As Manav sat in his office space, the AC room, sweating pathetically in front of Vamana, and everyone else on the virtual call, apologising profusely about what had just gone down, he saw in Vamana's eyes not anger but a reflection of his realisation. He saw Vamana put down whatever file he had in hand, take off his spectacles, and come closer to the camera.. "Manav, you are not the first start-up I have worked with, nor are you the only inexperienced over-achieving youngster I have met." Vamana was smiling, which confused Manav even more!

"Commitments are the face of your business, not mere words, Manav. When you make commitments, keep in mind all the circumstances that will work for or against your promise.

Measure it with sincere honesty and express the same. If you do not live up to your word, your skills mean little." Vamana had been kind in delivering his lesson.

This was a lot more than this one act of kindness had taught him about his arrogance and blind pursuit than anything else. Manav was humbled by the devastating strength of what a client can do to his confidence.

He left the virtual meeting, thinking of all the things he was going to say to his team. The office, on the other hand, was in complete silence this time too. They knew what a big deal the client had meant for the prospects of Avatar, and they knew how badly they had messed it up this time. Now, they waited in anticipation to see who Manav would fire, what he would say to them.

"I am sorry." Manav sat with his team on the next call and spoke patiently. The first words out of his mouth stunned them. "I pushed you too hard. I failed you as a leader and as a teammate. I did not respect you and your capacities. You did not let me down, you did not question me, and you did far more than I could have ever done. I am sorry. And I thank you for teaching me so much."

There were a few sobs and smiles in the room, for Manav's words had touched everyone. He went on to explain to them that he had called as many clients as possible on the way back to Avatar's office and personally apologised to each one of them, telling them about the honest timelines and committing, this time, with utter honesty, to keep them in the loop as things progressed.

Not only had Manav himself learnt the critical lesson of never over-committing and promising no matter how much the pressure, but also owning up to his mistake and doing whatever it takes to correct them. Whether he knew it or not, Manav had, for sure, earned a lot of respect from many of his teammates through the lesson that Vamana had taught him.

"I am sorry," he told Satrupa last, when all the calls had finished for the day and they had met along with Ved for dinner. "I overstepped. But you were patient and respectful. And you did not once refute my decisions in front of the team. I have a lot to learn from you." Ved was nodding in humble agreement. He could see why Manav was so confident about having Satrupa on board.

Moral - While setting eyes on the goals and in pursuit of bigger, better clients, it is extremely important not to lose sight of the ground reality. In the context of e-commerce and web-portals, when new experiments are being made and new territories explored, it will do well for an entrepreneur to take informed and educated steps and to only make promises after completely analysing the situation with pros and cons. In order to fish for larger clients, or more clients, start-ups often overstep their boundaries and capacities and demolish what could have been a slow but steady growth in the blind race of success. Building and growing a team go hand in hand with the growing business, and one must not jump at one without planning for the other.

Chapter 6

Ominous Opportunities

Coming back to the ground, slipping and falling, and making errors are a part of everyone's life. If someone says they have not fallen, made mistakes, often silly ones, and never messed up through their journey of growth, one of the three things is happening. Number one, and most common, is that they are lying to you. Number two, not so uncommon is that they have had no significant growth to speak of, and number three, the worst of them all, is that they are lying to themselves.

As an entrepreneur and leader, when the third happens, one has concocted for oneself the perfect and most straightforward and speedy recipe for self-destruction. For those lucky few who have the foresight and insight to review their errors or have close and reliable critics who can walk them through their mistakes, these moments of failure are opportunities for learning and growth.

With careful mentorship, such mistakes become stepping stones for long-term gains. However, not everyone is as fortunate. The first sign of destiny not favouring something happens when entrepreneurs are not even able to identify their errors. The next, more serious mistake is fearing the errors instead of learning from them. For un-mentored or misguided entrepreneurs, especially those with a low-risk faculty, mistakes can cripple away their risk-taking ability or the acumen to think beyond the ordinary.

Manav belonged to a category that was a mix of all experiences. He was lucky enough to know when he was making a mistake, he was privileged enough to have found people who were willing to help him and yet, he was possessed with a crippling fear of making mistakes one more time. In the last couple of months, Avatar has seen quite a roller-coaster ride.

Amidst an array of fame and acceptance, Manav had become the Icarus of ambition. He had tripled his planned sales and increased his user base by 70%. But things had begun to crumble when he could not deliver as per his commitment because of over-promising the capacity of his team. Vamana had taught him a lesson of committing only what he could deliver. Despite goofing up his delivery date and quality, Vamana had been genuine and supportive of Manav's sincerity because Manav had shown remorse and acceptance of his mistake immediately.

It had only been a miracle that his most influential client had given him a leeway instead of pulling back all contracts. If he had done that, not only would Manav have lost his biggest client, but also lost credibility and image in the market. It was then that the ambitious entrepreneur had been completely jolted out of his comfort zone, shaking his confidence and pushing him to a corner. Although he had learned a lesson of keeping a check on his pace and looking before leaping, the episode had left a deep insecurity in his mind.

"We have to rethink these numbers," Manav was found talking to Ved during a workout session. The sales team had pitched their quarterly targets that morning on the call, and so fresh from his first crash of ambition with Vamana, Manav was quite worried. He had looked more nervous than anything else at that time.

The team, as per Ved, had pitched a rather conservative number, keeping in mind the pace and scale Avatar had begun pulling. And yet, Manav could not seem to get back his momentum. "Let's take it slow. We have to keep our clients happy. If things go smoothly for the next year, then we will think about expanding." He was being extremely defensive and almost demotivating for his team.

That night, when he went for his routine walk where Satrupa joined him mid-way, she couldn't help but notice how his demeanour had been submissive in the several virtual meetings all day, just as it was distracted and slumped, even right now. Satrupa understood Manav more than anyone else and knew immediately what his dilemma must have been. But she also saw and understood not just Manav, the person she had grown to love, but also Manav the business owner, the rising entrepreneur, and the leader people looked up to at all times.

"Manav, look around you. Your sales team has closed in deals in the last month than any other business I have seen. Your design team is full of ideas, and my marketing vertical looks like they will burst open if no one asks them about their latest product campaign." Satrupa was practically giving Manav a shake—a much-deserved one, too.

Satrupa knew right now that she had to choose her words very carefully, between motivating Manav and reminding him of the responsibilities he owed to his team. But she couldn't simply watch him sink away into the abyss. What concerned her more than anything else was how confusing it would be for the team if they saw their leader oscillating between such highs and lows.

As a leader, it was Manav's role to be transparent and honest. Granted. But it was also extremely critical for him to portray an image of strength and clarity and of trust that he had in himself and his team. If Manav was not going to show that now, it would not only be demotivating for the team, but also affect the gravity of his leadership, because his crew would not take him seriously.

Ved and Satrupa had discussed it in Manav's absence, and Ved, as usual, had not minced his words about how he felt Manav was losing his head. "I know that if I talk to him, he is bound to get defensive. More critically, I feel that I may lose my calm and not be able to communicate with him the way he should be dealt with right now," Ved said.

Satrupa could understand where Ved was coming from. As someone who worked in an out-of-dynamics environment with communications, she was very well aware of the crisis people faced by spoiling situations that could have been handled well, simply by not being able to communicate efficiently. She responded, "Empathy is what he needs to deal with. This has to be empathy, not just for himself, but also his empathy for his team. I am confident I can invoke that faculty in Manav."

Satrupa was as wise as she was kind, which complemented her understanding of people's psyches quite well. It helped immensely that she had a very intimate bond with Manav, and her words were something he took seriously. This much she had come to understand. She nodded to Ved in a comforting look before logging off. She did not want Manav to know that she had been discussing him with Ved, not at this stage at least.

Later that night, when the duo logged in together to eat their dinner, Satrupa started by sharing her problems first.

"I don't know what's wrong, Manav. I tend to lose my temper easily these days. And I know that's a terrible thing to do because my team is looking up to me, and I need to set the best version of myself before them."

Manav, completely unaware of the context, gave his honest and well-meant advice.

"It must be frustrating. I understand. Come talk to me whenever you feel impatient. Maybe I can help you calm down. Don't ignore your mental health, but try to be sensitive to other people's experiences as well."

Just as Manav spoke these words, he realised he had been practicing pretty much the opposite of what he had been preaching.

Oh, God! Satrupa, what have I done! I have been behaving so unpredictably and indiscreetly with the entire Avatar team. It is so unfair to them!

The gravity of his conduct in the last couple of weeks was dawning upon Manav, making him feel rather stupid about himself at the moment.

Satrupa knew this was the right moment to cheer him up.

"This is a great experience of learning, Manav! It is such a wonderful blessing that you are being able to learn a critical lesson with a really small price to pay at such an early stage of your enterprise!"

Satrupa's words had a positive twist in her signature style. She continued, seeing that she had Manav's attention and interest.

"I know things went south for us, and we touched the dark water. But we're back. We have learned our lesson, and we would be extremely stupid to not make the best of it."

This is when she told Manav that Ved had also been concerned about Manav's attitude in the last month. After all, Manav had been rejecting all growth plans, increased his one-on-one interaction with existing clients to the level where he had begun micro-managing every response and feedback. This dip had left the team even more confused than they had been during his last oscillation into the sky!

Satrupa explained with a kindness in her voice that this was just the right time to bring about a significant shift in the ambience. If something wasn't done fast enough, Avatar—as a concept, a team, and a brand—was probably heading for a hit they may not be able to recover from.

It was getting more and more obvious in the market space that the coronavirus was here to stay, and the world would have to adapt itself into a digital revolution to keep pace with how people had gotten used to living. Online transactions, access, and service availability had skyrocketed.

Manav had foreseen this future long before many large e-commerce entrepreneurs. He had catered to the futuristic needs of small-scale enterprises to go online. However, now that there was proof of concept—and rather a rage—competition had started sprouting from all places, offering versions derived from Avatar's model.

Amidst this was a smart and vicious businessman named Hiranya Kashyap, infamously known among funders as HK. Not only had he blatantly aped Avatar's model, but he had also been trying to poach their existing clients using the same techniques, targeting Avatar's audience segment far more aggressively—because he had a lot of money to burn.

What made matters worse was that the quality of HK's product was nowhere near Avatar's. Their portal crashed with increased traffic, looked nearly identical for all businesses, lacked automation and customization, and to top it off, they charged about 40% more!

But the thing about marketing is that it makes a product creep into the minds and hearts of consumers. Before you realise it, there's a solid brand recall and association. In such cases, when a need arises, the media consumer turns into a hot lead simply because the effort of conversion has already been done through brand saturation.

With HK's rising popularity, Avatar risked losing market edge and authenticity. Unlike traditional business, which is based on years of trust and relationship building, online consumption depends heavily on ease of access, visibility, effortlessness, promptness, and quality assurance.

Another thing Manav had learned early on: the online marketplace is far more cost-effective, due to the elimination of several unwanted overheads. He had cracked the code of affordability, making online services appealing to traditionally set-up businesses. And now HK was trying to overthrow this, simply with a vulgar display of money and invasive advertising.

If Manav didn't take control now, everything would be for nothing—his job loss, the risk-taking, the innovation—it would all be lost to aggressive competitors.

That's when Manav decided to come out of his shell of insecurity and act.

"People, I think we have to find a middle ground. Between going blind with aggression and simply playing on the back foot, there's got to be an informed and educated way of doing this."

Manav was addressing his team leads while scrolling through his professional social media feed for the latest in tech and web commerce. Avatar was still cutting-edge with its customised, cost-effective services. But to stay competitive, Manav knew he needed to diversify—offer more services, improve reach, and retain customers longer.

More importantly, the marketing team had been focusing only on B2C (Business-to-Customer).

"I think we can reach a higher scale and visibility with B2B or business-to-business connections."

Manav was beginning to open his mind again. Satrupa and Ved filled him in on team discussions.

"We should reach out to curators, art experts, panellists, and reviewers who can help with membership and subscription models for their groups. This way, we get a massive reach and also go in-depth with community building and word of mouth!"

These were brilliant ideas. Manav could see the team was gearing up for a better version of Avatar.

"So, that brings us back to the question that has been a bit of a sore spot for you all this while. Manav, with the new strategy, we need more techies and a few more experts in PR and Business Development," Ved explained in a calm and assuring tone.

Manav raised his eyebrows, almost about to retreat into his shell again, when he got distracted by a message online.

"Dear Manav," it said, "We do not know each other personally, but I have been a colleague of Vamana for a while. He told me about your enterprise, which triggered me to break out to you and discuss a possibility."

It was from someone named Narasimha. He was talking about remote work options for his apprentices.

"The guy runs a skill development program."

Manav scoffed. He had been looking to hire, but Avatar needed pedigree—sharp, smart, experienced professionals, especially with e-commerce embedded within highly customised portals.

"I get his mission and all, but this is not for us. We need crisp, smart, and experienced people, especially now that we can afford it."

Manav nodded from side to side, but his body language was telling another story. Ved noticed.

"But you are conflicted in that claim, aren't you?"

He had known Manav for a long time and understood where he was coming from.

"I know we've been brought up thinking pedigree matters—the best institutes, the best organisations, the best locality… that's why our mind tells us to seek the same when we go out to hire."

Satrupa, quiet till now, finally spoke.

"What about you guys? Both of you come from very average backgrounds. You have no elite degree or work experience to speak of. Should I then assume that you know nothing about your work?"

Manav listened and, almost subconsciously, began scanning Narasimha's profile. It had stories of people from all walks of life. He had spent a large part of his career building others' careers.

Most of Narasimha's apprentices had found good work in the start-up space. Manav was intrigued. He decided—out of sheer curiosity—to find out what was behind this mysterious success.

What could he possibly be teaching them that transforms their lives? He thought as he set up an appointment.

"I cannot connect with you in the morning or at night, but I think I can manage an evening," Narsimha said to him on a call. "I take morning and night classes for people who are working, and so I am always occupied at that time."

Thus, the duo arranged a virtual meet since no city or spot was working out for either of them.

"Neither land nor water is needed to get where we want now," Narsimha was engaging in what looked like small talk, but was his candid, child-like fascination. "Can you imagine how access and information are changing with this virtual world? Our perceptions are being overhauled, our capacities being revised. It's almost like a whole new world!"

Narsimha was getting at the deeper purpose of his work. "Which is why I realise that the more we excavate and explore, the more our prejudices are broken down, the horizon of our mindset broadened."

Manav was listening intently, almost mesmerised by Narsimha's storytelling. He went on to explain how he had been super-elite, working only with the clouds and above. But he had transformed into this bizarre, most unconventional form because his prejudices had been broken by people who had shown unconditional devotion and sincerity.

"There was this young professional called Prahlad. He had wanted to work with me on an AI project for a long time. But he was a nobody! How could I randomly hire him? I brought on people only from Ivy Leagues and whatnot!"

Narsimha recounted Prahlad's persistence in sending his papers, models, and theories to him endlessly.

"Earlier, I would ignore him, hoping he would give up and leave. I did not even open a single file or document he had sent. But nothing wore him down."

Narsimha narrated how he finally gave in and checked out Prahlad's model on AI for medical assistance. He had been blown away by the sheer insightfulness of the approach and how meticulous his steps were.

"He changed my perspective towards pedigree—towards the prejudice of hiring people based on the stamps they carry. I then decided to start working with unknown people, people who did not belong to any category, any specific pedigree, but had, in their sense, great insight, experience, and intellect to speak for. The results amazed me. The grassroots, hand-scrubbing insight is so valuable and under-valued."

Manav was soaking it all in and firing questions because he could not resist digging deeper, as though this was some kind of salvation for his lack of privileges.

"And then, I am assuming you train them on some skills and redirect them as new people?"

Narsimha smiled. "That was one of my early prejudices, too. Those that the ones without any stamps will need polishing. They don't!"

He explained to Manav how he had initially tried to start with his students on a new tech-space and business models.

"But they were well-versed with that. The internet had brought everything in front of their eyes, and they were perceptive enough to read."

The only thing Narsimha then had to do was evaluate their capabilities through live project testing across industries, give them visibility through consultancy opportunities, and boom! They were breaking out of the shells of their labels and fitting right into their expected forms, giving inputs and insights from the grassroots level, introducing notions that first-world entitled individuals had never even thought about.

"You would understand that, more than anyone else. After all, you do not have a pedigree and must know the struggles yourself. Now is your chance to make your enterprise stronger and to create an impact that goes beyond business..."

It had been a month since their first meeting. Manav and Narsimha had been working very closely since then. Manav had hired a whole set of consultants from Narsimha's network. These were women and men from all professions, geographies, and age groups. And he was more than happy with the results.

"The end-user insight is so strong. The exposure and experience are so valuable that we end up saving a lot of time in research and development."

Although the pace matched Manav's comfort level for the most part, he still felt that Narsimha was sometimes getting a little too aggressive for his control. In Manav's mind, there was an objective, a budget, and a target curve that his team designed quarter after quarter.

While Narsimha's resource pool met those needs, there was a sense of urgency in him—an untamed fire, driven by his passion to do good—that sometimes overwhelmed the calculated pace and structure Avatar had set. In a couple of meetings where Narsimha and Manav had pitched together, Manav had noticed that clients were getting intimidated by Narsimha's intensity and powerful approach.

But thankfully, before things spiralled, a woman stepped into the picture.

Her name was Simhani. As far as Manav could tell, she was a stakeholder in Narsimha's enterprise. But she seemed to hold significant influence over his affairs. Manav assumed someone on the team must have tipped her off about Narsimha's intensity and the risk it posed during client interactions.

This is when she stepped in and put a lid on the matter before things got out of control.

"Narsimha will be moving around for another project. So I will be taking over for him now," she said in a cool, calculated tone that burned with a quiet fire—even Narsimha was visibly subdued.

This was an old habit of the good man—to get carried away with passion—at which point Simhani would intervene to pull him back before he harmed his reputation or that of his organisation, built on dedication and goodwill.

The transfer of power and participation did not affect their relationships—neither between Narsimha and Simhani, nor between them and Manav. It was a great example of how power dynamics could be balanced and managed.

Manav had learned his lessons well and was sure he would complete the loop of learning by doing his part to pass on the experience he had gained.

A few days later, Manav was discussing projects with some of his clients when they asked about dedicated resources for their work.

"You just have to look close enough. There's talent, wisdom, and expertise in people all around you—in shapes and forms you may not have imagined. It is only a matter of breaking the pillars of prejudice and keeping an open mind."

Manav was wiser, once again, for having understood and acknowledged his mistakes. This made him a lot more confident—and more often than not, deeply reflective about what other mistakes he could still learn from.

Moral - There's insight, intellect, and valuable experience in people around us, in backgrounds that we may not have been conditioned to look at or even expect. As a path-breaking entrepreneur, working in a space that is experimental, complex, and especially in aspects that deal with e-commerce, money matters, a bottom-up approach of concept understanding helps to design your product from the point of view of the end user. Instead of putting on an elite lens of judgement, if you want to hire talent, look at the kind of projects the individuals have worked on, the hurdles they have overcome and that,

perhaps, will help you, as a leader and an entrepreneur, to build a team that is solid, grounded and ambitious in ways that privileges cannot bring.

Chapter 7

Working for the Bigger Good and Goal

The most rewarding and worthwhile endeavours, the ones that leave a mark not just on your bank account but on the world, are a lot like that rare dish where the spices all play in harmony. It is not easy to create, or easy to find. One needs to put in much of their heart and soul. It is that constant striving to do the best, most impactful thing that keeps one grounded, that lends integrity, and that, ultimately, elevates the entire operation.

As an entrepreneur, as a leader, and most importantly, as a human being, Manav had begun to learn this. In the last year of his growth with Avatar, he had tasted his share of spices - the tang of inspiration, the bitterness of mistakes, the sharp zest of competition, the rich flavour of success.

And while he sometimes stumbled with the ingredients, he always managed to find the perfect balance, often guided by the wisdom he was lucky enough to attract to his life. Take the last set of learnings, for instance.

He had been randomly pinged by a philanthropic enabler called Narsimha, who changed his perspective about how resources and especially people could be discovered and honed from any walk of life, instead of simply looking for high pedigree.

Manav had also learned, the hard way, from Simhani that there has to be a balancing and controlling factor more than anything else in the pursuit of success and handling failures.

And though his path was now set, a clear road ahead, he still had the invaluable map.

Although Manav was certain that he had dipped into many instances of failures, in the concoction, along the way, he had also tasted success. His success, albeit very fresh and young, was both appreciable for his position and very well-deserved for the kind of struggles and hard work he had put in.

With the customer base expanded from local businesses in Vaikuntha to neighbouring cities, to other major cities in the state, and finally reaching a national scale and fame, Avatar had grown exponentially. And now, with international clients knocking on his door, Manav felt the thrilling pressure of a conductor leading a global orchestra.

Manav had just bagged his first couple of international clients who had reached out to him on their own, because of his work with one of the most prestigious universities in India, in their subscription model of online portal services for education. "Word of mouth is the key, Satrupa. We have to keep our customers happy, and even in that, the more hot-shot and influential our customer, the better their reach will be, and therefore our visibility will find a whole new level of impact in the global market."

Manav was charged up ever since the contract had been finalized. Some of the bigger clients in India had also become a major share of his portfolio, who had signed up for premium services. "Avatar is making its mark everywhere now. When people think of creative, customizable web services, they will only think of Avatar."

Ved nodded with a smile, but always, the more conscious part of Manav's thinking, his smile was neither heartfelt nor convincing. As usual, instead of directly hammering Manav with his concerns, he had learned the new trick of deliberating with Satrupa about them.

He had understood now that he was not very good with the impact of his words, and therefore, seeking consultation from Satrupa not only helped him preserve his relationship with his best friend but also taught him immensely about the right approach to conversations with anyone.

"What is a good way to check how much is too much?' Ved asked Satrupa in front of Manav, with a context that was not far removed from the problem he was trying to solve with Manav.

"My sales team wants some infrastructural support, and when I asked them to send me a proposition, they sent me a budget for tech support that is not going down well with my understanding. What do you think, Satrupa?" Ved's question was an engaging one, and even though it was talking about a specific issue, it would help to address a universal confusion that could be used to answer many such puzzles.

"Well, the ideal thing would be to first assess priorities on expenditure and then simply study the return of probable investments. With some margin, of course." Satrupa had worked with several media platforms, and that is exactly how their evaluation worked.

In print costs, air times, and outdoor strategies, it was always about evaluating what and how much you would get in return. This conversation gave her a perfect opportunity to slide in her concern with Manav as well.

"We have been spending quite a lot on marketing, Manav. I think we can better use that money in places where it is needed. You are well aware that Ved has been trying to make budget cuts wherever possible."

Every time Manav threw in a flamboyant demand, an appealing but one expensive idea of ads, features, or even resources, Ved had to jump in to negotiate for the bare minimum requirements, cutting down the extravaganza wherever possible. He knew that Manav's heart was in the right place. It was not that he was trying to do anything fancy for himself. That was never the aim.

Ever since the team had grown, they had to accommodate a lot of space for setting up, storage, and even occasional meetings. Because of this, as much as Ved requested, Manav had moved out of his apartment to make room for the office space.

Despite getting into a comfortable situation financially, Manav still maintained a humble standing for himself. After having moved out of Ved's apartment, Manav still lived in a humble one-bedroom house and dressed as simply as he used to, except when he had to meet high-profile clients to make a pitch or address a talk or webinar.

Satrupa also understood where he was coming from when he wanted to create a social media image with good marketing strategies. Manav wanted quality, and he wanted the quality to be known.

"There are so many companies that offer simple website services and charge a bomb for worthless products and even worse services. We are here making the real impact." Manav always reinstated the one rule amongst all the team members of Avatar. "No matter what, we never compromise with our quality and we never cheat our customers," he would say every time he addressed his employees.

It was perhaps these principles that had brought Manav to the position of success and consistent growth. However, there seemed to be a key element he seemed to be forgetting. Like a pomegranate seed stuck at the back of his tooth, he knew there was something, perhaps very tiny, that he was skipping or forgetting, but he couldn't quite put a finger on it.

"Eh, if it is important, it will come back to me on its own!" He would exclaim to Ved during their long walks, when they felt like discussing new ideas or diving deeper into some idea, beyond the walls of the office space.

Ever since Avatar hit the international market, it has sort of become a trend for several people to keep reaching out to him with different agendas. Some media persons wanted a bite, controversial or otherwise. Professionals were looking for job opportunities, companies seeking possible partnerships, venture capitalists, and some random leeches who were old acquaintances or had dissed Manav for his radical thinking or 'dreamy ideas'.

But now, everyone wanted a piece of his success. "We have to be a lot more selective about who we give access to," Satrupa demanded after a particularly harrowing gentleman who had been given an appointment without much diligence. "He was not requesting but demanding that I give him a portal for his specific needs. When I explained to him the packages, he glared at me. Even when I was finishing up, trying to be as polite as possible, he kept saying, 'You owe me this!' I am never getting into unvetted meetings like that again!"

Manav was listening to Satrupa complain, making mental notes about the better briefing and screening process with the sales team. But he could feel that old nagging feeling at the back of his head rising even more intently right now. "We have to appoint and prepare some presentations and representatives to go to the e-commerce convention happening at the cyber conference of the World Revolution Forum. I was right all along about the futuristic way being conducting online webinars and conferences, the way things are moving towards the future!"

Manav was irritated for some reason, although he couldn't figure out what it was.

The irritation was more for not knowing what was going on in his head than anything else at all. "Anyway, let's polish our deck to match the conference theme- Simplifying the Online Space," he said and walked away to meet another client. Even though Manav had moved out, he still hung out more often than not at Ved's house, in the office space. He said it made him a lot more productive. But truth be told, it soothed something in his soul. Like a compass always pointing home, no matter what his adventures and the destination. He remembered Ved teasing him about this, though he did not show it.

Manav's resolution to step out and interact with more people, engaging in diversity, was almost answered by the design of the conference. As per the invitation sent to Avatar, there would be a teaming up of two individuals who necessarily did not know each other and were participating in the conference, to be each other's partner during all events and contests in the conference. This would include all internal team members as well as all registered guests.

As it would turn out, their sales and marketing head, who was managing the conference, Renuka, had been selected to register along with Manav for the conference. They had touched base once before the actual commencement and briefed each other about their backgrounds.

Renuka had told him about her role in the conference and also enquired about his aspirations for the event. While communicating on one of the conference's pre-designed platforms, Manav had told her about the significance of this opportunity. This was going to be all about pitching Avatar as a cutting-edge solution for bigger players, who wanted an online, hassle-free e-commerce experience for their many businesses.

"The idea is that for giant corporations, managing each of the segments of e-commerce is confusing and complicated. With Avatar, we have in-built integration systems to ensure that all payment gateways, financial analysis, and transaction platforms can be either broken down into individual chapters or amalgamated into a singular platform, depending on whether you want exclusive or inclusive accounting," Manav said.

This was going to be a revolutionary step, as far as e-commerce was concerned. Earlier, businesses that had gotten used to their online transactions would have everything converted to the online platform. For singular businesses and platforms, it worked out well. However, where things got complicated was the extremes on the spectrum. For small businesses, it was not possible to have all transactions online, owing to the unorganized sector involved in many ways, or smaller transactions for their target audience, for which the online space was still not accessible to that extent.

Manav's payment gateways were allowing integration of both online and offline payment modes to still fall into the same accounting setups, thus making matters simple. On the other hand, much larger organizations were running as umbrella brands and had multiple independent platforms online. The trick would be to integrate all of their payments into a single platform to make the experience seamless and inviting as a one-stop solution for all.

"We also offer consolidated theme and process options for multi-branching within the same umbrella brand to keep consistency in branding," Manav was explaining to someone who was impressed with layouts that were playing flawlessly on the screen. With the new team that had come in through the Narasimha network and advice, Avatar's insight in product building for the end user and business management had enhanced miraculously because they had now been able to tap into the needs of the customer and build the website customization based on the needs of the users. This had impressed several clients who wanted more than just a pretty-looking site.

It was when there was a little tea break that Renuka joined his breakout room, where random, informal interactions were happening, and introduced him to a tall, strong-looking gentleman, dressed a little too humbly for the elite setting around him.

Manav was already creating a bias against him in his head, profiling him as a potential leech, but his thoughts were interrupted when Renuka introduced him as Parshuram, her husband. "What! This guy is Parshuram?" Manav's mind was echoing in disbelief. Who had not heard of the multi-billionaire? Parshuram was a smart and aggressive Venture Capitalist who could be counted among the ten most influential people in the world in the last 10 years.

However, more than his business accomplishments and acquisitions, Parshuram was famous for his philanthropic bent of mind, for his new and innovative projects, and most lovingly, for his no-stakes funding contest for humanitarian businesses. He was, in fact, here at this convention scouting for the next potential opportunities to support.

"Manav, it is so awesome to finally meet you. I have been reading about how you have been working hard to change the way online businesses access and relevance are changing for small-scale businesses. That's a true and well-appreciated example of a bottom-up approach for the masses, Manav. I am sure you are proud of yourself for this!" he said.

It was as though someone had opened the door of a giant dam, and Manav had been standing at its entrance. Parshuram's firm and subtle smile, his exploring, non-judgmental gaze, and his words had pierced Manav right to the point in his soul, which had been itching him with a constant nag in the last few months. He did not even pretend to smile, to accept Parshuram's compliment, if at all it was one.

Manav was overpowered with guilt and remorse as the realization hit him about why he had been uneasy. "Mr. Parshuram. I wish I could say I deserve even a quarter of the praise you have just bestowed upon me. I think I understand very well why you have chosen to join me and talk to me like this. And for this, I am thankful and humbled."

Manav felt his eyes tearing up a little, and he couldn't even try to fight off the flooding of his emotions right now. "Would you like to step away to a private chat room and have a cup of tea with me?" Parshuram offered in the most candid, non-pretentious voice Manav had heard from the big shots.

Manav understood now why Renuka had taken so much interest in his work and why she had brought Parshuram into personal contact. She had seen what Manav had failed to perceive about his own business. He was immediately indebted to her perceptiveness and prompt action to bring her husband into contact with Manav, with hopes that his words would be able to guide the man back to the right track.

The duo, with Renuka at their side, silently absorbing all that was going on, stepped into a private chat space designed for one-on-one interactions and liaising purposes. They settled in and took a couple of minutes to bring their cups of tea to their respective desks. Manav was so quiet on the outside that he felt his insides would burst open with all the chaos that was going on inside his mind.

Parshuram put a comforting face on and spoke softly, "Do not hesitate, my friend. You do not have to worry about what I think or feel. I have been labelled into categories so many times that I have learned not to look at anyone with judgment."

Manav saw a completely vulnerable and honest look in his eyes, making him feel that the man on the high pedestal was just another human being, with his share of struggles and mistakes. Renuka, looking at how shaken Manav was, nudged him to pick up his cup of tea and started making some small talk. "I love the virtual soothing environment they have created for enabling candid conversations! The yellow blossoms that look like a generous bunch of grapes remind me of my childhood when I used to think that these were edible fruits!"

Everyone laughed at that because apparently, everyone could relate to that experience.

"Childhood was a special time, right? Things were simple. There were no burdens and one was only limited by school timings, the rest was a blank canvas for imagination," Parshuram also added, looking somewhere into space and smiling.

"It was also a time when thoughts and actions were not corrupt," Manav spoke after a dash of silence. He was finally feeling stable enough to start talking.

"When I used to sit in that shoddy bank office building, with patches of paint falling off, squeaking chairs, and malfunctioning AC, I met people from all walks of life, walking in with their dreams to build something for themselves, an enterprise, a future. And I would feel frustrated at the time because more often than not, I couldn't help them out," Manav recalled his motivation to help the old lady who had wanted to set up shop with her son.

He had wanted to help out small businesses, people whose dreams were crushed by the norms and profit margins of the giant corporations. Which is why he had started Avatar, which could allow online visibility, transactions, and interactions for small-scale businesses on a subscription model. It was to help those who had neither the expertise, the exposure, nor the finances to afford such a platform.

"Initially, when I started working on the theory, I explored the various options available in the digital space for website development. They would all charge exorbitantly and not provide the customised services that small-scale or starting businesses would need. More importantly, there was no guidance for business growth and support." Manav was talking candidly about the very nerve he had planned on touching with his enterprise.

Parshuram wanted Manav to internalise and accept the agony he was talking about right now. "What happened along the way?" Manav smiled at this question, a sarcastic, scoffing, almost bitter smile.

"Success happened, Sir. Avatar hit the news, and we started making profits. We started playing in the bigger league, and then, I lost track of everything Avatar was supposed to be about, and I sold myself to the economy of power." Manav had not even touched his tea.

"That happens to most of us. Please take my word for it. I have seen a whole buffet of businesses get lost in the mist of glory." Parshuram was kind and thoughtful in his words and expressions.

"But I would say, you are very lucky to see, so early on in your journey, about what you're missing. Most of us do not even reflect till it's too late, till we are too deep in it and have lost our dreams and passion to the race."

Manav nodded, remembering categorically loathing large businesses that had changed their strategies and priorities over time to cater to the power of economics. He was diving into a bout of guilt again when he saw Parshuram share his screen and draw out Avatar's first business report.

"Look at these couple of quarters, when you had just started. Check out the number of businesses you had supported back then. Look at how consistent they have been in keeping their subscriptions and bringing you new clients. Before coming to the convention, I had pulled data about potential people I might want to work with. Your name had popped up in my search. Do you see this massive spike in financial growth? This is how much those businesses have grown and profited ever since you gave them Avatar. That's just a trailer of the potential it holds for doing so much good!" Parshuram was smiling.

Renuka was smiling, and Manav found himself smiling too. Instead of pinpointing everything he had messed up, Parshuram had pointed out the merits and potential of Avatar's intent. It was like Manav's brain had turned a page, which had entirely different notes written on it!

"We can get back there. For the larger clients we have acquired, it would be unfair to let them off. We can appoint a dedicated team to handle the large clients. That will keep a backup income flowing. But let's turn to our original motto. Let's work with clients with humble needs. I know profit will be slow initially, but with the quality and efficiency we offer, we will be able to reach the scale. We already see so many applications, even right now!" Manav was mentally mapping the next steps.

He was hopeful and felt like a burden had been lifted off his chest. This was the best he had felt in a long time. He thanked Parshuram and Renuka for their kindness, specifically Renuka for being the mediating force in introducing them and Parshuram for his kindness and attention.

"We'll be seeing more of each other, Manav. Very soon, someone will be reaching out to you to help with your operations." Parshuram got up and left, bidding goodbye, thanking Manav for a delicious cup of tea.

Manav smiled his original and honest smile after a long time, and turned out to discuss with Renuka what the next steps were going to be.

Moral - The essence of a business is not its service, its high and mighty branding, or even its long list of clients. The true soul of a business is the good it does, even in the process of being profitable. As a rising entrepreneur, it is easy and common to lose sight of the good you had set out to do. But it is important to keep bringing yourself back to the original truth and track. Not just because it feels ethically right, but also because, if you get distracted from the original objective, uproot the aim that anchored the enterprise, it becomes vulnerable to the swaying storm of the industry and can potentially be swayed away and drowned in every passing trend and norm. This is not just bad for the business perception but also an operational disaster. Keep a clear head, focus on the roots of your intentions, and keep an open mind to keep revisiting your actions.

Chapter 8

Sticking to the Principles

When you reach a certain stage in business, as you do in life, the broader flow of things becomes your main focus. It so happens, if you observe closely, that the flow goes into slow motion and you can extrapolate every element and assess the significance, priority, and ultimately, the decisions based on the compromises you are willing to make for the larger good or the bigger negotiations. These are potentially uncomfortable situations for an entrepreneur when taking the right call, which is right both for the business as well as the product and its consumers, is not a black and white decision. That is the true test of mettle.

And this is a test not only of how intelligent or wise, or experienced your acumen is, but also a test of your principles and roots, which are supposedly the foundation of your enterprise. These struggles come into the lives of all entrepreneurs, at least all of those who are creating a large-scale impact in some way.

Manav had been climbing to this level of impact and effect gradually and steadily. And naturally, he had begun with the first encounters of such a dilemma. In the past, he had struggled with finding focus and rethinking his market and priorities. He had also fallen and learnt from his mistakes over commitment and balance of scaling and over-reaching, as compared to underachieving. In most of those cases, he had been fortunate enough to find some or the other form of guidance from people and experiences from different domains and expertise.

These episodes had been more like a switch to prompt him back in the right direction and to simply highlight the mistakes he may have been making. Ever since the world conference, Manav had kept in constant touch with Renuka and Parshuram and sought constant guidance from them about his approach, or whenever he struggled in making the right decision for the business that would not hamper his path for the larger vision.

However, the game was changing now. More than simply pointing pins and needles in the process, the process now would be reflection-heavy, and it would take more than the flip of a switch to get to the right track. Manav was not aware of the arising crisis yet, but he was about to fall into a pit in which, if nothing else, he would need a lot of time and patience with reflections.

The phone had been buzzing incessantly. Manav had been occupied with setting up Avatar's first convention, 'Redefining Online Access'. There were people from all industries joining in to take a look at the services available in the online space. But additionally, to not make it look like a sales conference, it was imperative to invite several different kinds of case studies, business ideas, and tech development that would seem relevant to the clients. But there were a lot of clashes coming up in planning, execution, and, more importantly, prioritisation.

Manav was getting in a fix about a few technical issues, now and then. Most of these issues were being solved simply by evaluating the equation from a higher-risk, higher investment standpoint. But Ved walked in with a troubled look on his face that even Manav could not decode as easily as the rest of the 'tricky ones'.

"Manav, there's something we need to discuss."

The duo went into the office room where one of the session plans was being set up for later. There was a man from the event management, Ram, who was deciding on some breakout charts. This man seemed meticulously involved in picking the right set of people to be placed together for each and every session. Amidst the last-minute preparations, there was also chaos and a crisis in introducing products to some of the more prominent clients.

"The problem, Manav, is that more than one client is looking for the same kind of portal for e-commerce services, and we do not have enough mock-ups ready to show different designs." Ved sounded a little too harrowed.

This meant that he had already tried all options before bringing this up with Manav. "We have checked with the design team, we have scanned through all the dummies we have, and we have even tried to modify some of our existing designs on the sandbox, but they just won't work as 'customised' for those looking for unique portals."

Manav fell silent for a couple of minutes, tapping his pen on his forehead, racing his mind as he paced back and forth in the room, crossing the breakout session charts in the 3-D design of the flowchart of the conference. He stopped there, examining closely.

"I think I know what we can do. We can use the same portal for both clients, just by changing around the colour schemes and layout just a little bit, without really affecting the sitemap." Ved had a big question mark on his face. Because that is what he had just explained as a part of the problem.

"Let me explain," Manav took over the space near the 3-D layout, addressing the gentleman working on the seating.

"Excuse me, sir, you are, I am assuming, the man responsible for the arrangements and logistics? My name is Manav and you are...?"

The man turned around to smile at him, a big, kind, and wise smile. "Hi, Manav. I have been observing your work, talking to your team for a long time. It is great to finally meet you in person. My name is Ram."

For some reason, the moment Manav shook his hand, he felt something change inside him. He felt that he had met this man before. In another look, in another form maybe, but I met him before. Still dazed from the encounter, he tried to focus back on his objective.

"So Ram, correct me if I am wrong, but you are helping us fit the right set of people for the right session, which will be happening simultaneously in each of these sections, right?" Seeing Ram nod, he continued to Ved.

"So, all we have to do is make sure that the two clients are appointed to two different sessions happening simultaneously in two different rooms. If we do that, there will be no duplicity and we will still get away with two happy clients!"

Ved was starting to see his point. But being his diligent self, he wanted to make sure they had all corners covered. "Are you sure we will be able to place them effectively, and they will not interact with the subject later?"

He had a valid point, but that is when Manav turned around to Ram to suggest. "We have to create a distraction, Ram, some attractive trophy hunt, say a golden deer, so to speak, that can be chased and will keep the two set away from each other."

Ram looked like he was getting the point of all of this. "So you would want me to create a chase and to pursue it with them. And it would be a distraction to make sure whatever your objective is, it does not clash?"

Manav nodded, somewhat ashamed of what he was asking a random stranger to do. There was something about Ram, though, something inherently glowing and righteous that made me hesitant to be so forthright about his treachery with the man.

"What do you think?" He asked Ram involuntarily, only realising later that he was subconsciously seeking the man's approval.

Ram looked at him without judgment or prejudice. He smiled again and answered with utter honesty. "Manav, as an outsider, the perception of Avatar is that of a game-changer. It is a business that matters and has brought a true and honest meaning to business, especially for those who have been duped before."

Manav sat down to listen patiently, knowing that despite the time crisis, he needed this prompt to make a decision that was not very black and white. Ram continued, "Managing a few more clients is just one part of the game. Protecting the vision, the very soul of Avatar, that's what is needed as well."

Ram continued, "Before managing some of the largest events in the history of India, and in turn, changing how events are perceived in the corporate space, I used to work on the marketing side of the business. I have, as a representative of corporations, many times been pitched several different stories, and faced many different tough decisions. Once, an agency had cancelled giving us a contract at the last moment on account of a prior commitment to someone else."

Ram recalled his past experiences one after another. "Another time, there was a law firm trying to burn bridges between me and another family business run by my brother Lakshman. I have had to identify and weed out so many usurpers and intruders that it was almost tiring."

Manav could relate to that. Back in the banking days, so many people came with false applications or false reasons for defaulting, trying to get away with anything. In those times, Manav would feel cheated, insulted, and often frustrated. He would complain to Ved during their tea breaks, "You know what pinches the most? A lot of them, when you look deeper, have genuine problems. But if only they would come clean, it would not be so pathetic!"

As he heard Ram talk about his challenges, Manav was reminded of all those moments of deceit. His thoughts were brought back to Ram's words when he heard him say, "All those times, I felt that it would be so much easier if the service providers were not lying. I would understand. I would even help them out. If only they were honest to their word!"

This sounded like such a heartfelt and honest discussion that Manav did not mind giving up his work for a bit. It seemed to him that Ram came from a place in his heart that, along with honest insight, also had a lot of experience. Perhaps the way he helped others overcome greed for profit was what was so tempting. There was something about him that did not fit the picture, though.

Manav had tracked the man's profile and noticed that he had been a prominent business owner several years ago and then disappeared for 14 years, without any trace or news. Rumour said that it had something to do with his controversy in the family business. Some said he was trying to deceive his brother, while others said that his brother deceived him.

Irrespective of who was at fault, Ram had disappeared from the business grid for more than a decade. He had resurfaced only a couple of years ago, in a case of business acquisition. He had taken over a rather malicious entrepreneur's empire.

Ravan had been infamous in the industry for his unethical ways of running the business, especially in the way that he treated women. Manav learned later that Ravan had been working with Sita, who was a close friend and associate of Ram.

When Ravan had tried to harass Sita, who, although a strong and independent HR professional herself, had felt extremely harrowed because of the experience and reached out to Ram for support. It was that which had brought Ram out of his incognito mode, and that is when he had come at Ravan with all his force and resources, to take over his empire in Lanka.

It was perhaps this and everything else that Ram had endured and fought for; many say that he was deeply in love with Sita, whom he had to eventually part with because of a difference in opinions, which had made Ram so deep and patient and so honourable in his outlook on life.

Even though Manav knew none of that at this point when they were standing in the office, having this conversation, he was intrigued, and rightfully so. They said it was impossible to have met Ram, spoken to him, and left without any impact on one's life.

Ram's words kept echoing in his ears as Manav quickly set out to arrange a call with his clients. "You will be seeing them tomorrow anyway, Manav. Can't this wait till then? We have a lot of things to finish before tomorrow morning!" Ved was concerned that such rushed discussions would bring no good.

"I understand, Ved. But we will work through this. But I believe this is what has to be done at the earliest." He gestured to Ved to be quiet with a finger on his lips and turned out to respond on the video call as the client's end connected.

"Hello, Mr. Vibhishan. Thank you for making time at such short notice." Manav, after listening to all of Ram's stories and experiences, had decided that he had to do the right thing. Almost a year and a half ago, when he had spent many nights chalking down documents for the deck of Avatar, for deciding and designing its mission, vision, and core values, he had thought about all the good he would be doing and the satisfaction he would be bringing to himself and the people who worked with him.

"Friends, somewhat may, do not ever forget the founding values of Avatar: transparency, excellence, and empathy," Manav had addressed his employees month after month, in every all-hands session or group discussion. It was written in bold, golden letters when you entered the office, too, as a reminder to anyone who risked forgetting it.

"And yet, I forgot all about them under stress," he had thought to himself while dialling in.

But now, it was time to be as honest and humble as possible. He explained to Vibhishan the situation as it was, that they had a crisis of design, but their thoughts were clear on the product, and they wanted to deliver only the best.

"Would it be possible for you to take control of the project and help us with a little time so we can give you something you deserve?" Manav's forthright honesty came as a rare and pleasant surprise to Vibhishan.

"I appreciate your transparency, Manav, and I am so glad you brought up the crisis before it became an irreversible problem."

Manav ended the call far more relieved than he had felt in a long time. He made a couple of similar calls to the few other clients who were going to be hit because of the crisis.

"We will make sure that you like the mock-ups we share tomorrow. The advantage would be that you will be able to give us any feedback about what you would like to be different from the existing platform," He was explaining to the last client before signing off. Manav had received positive responses from almost all clients, and from the ones he did not, he was resolved to win them over during the conference with a better deal and confidence.

All this while, Satrupa had been so busy handling the press releases, the launch materials, and media packages that she had no idea about what was going on in Manav's head. When he finally came to her, after resolving the issue and completing the calls, she appreciated him for his honesty, all the while thinking about what she would have done had she been in Manav's place.

Weighing in all the options, she still could not make up her mind, even though she was just as invested and just as passionate about Avatar. After mulling over the thought for a long time, Satrupa decided to let it go. That was another wonderful thing about her. Knowing Manav's quirks and unpredictable actions, it was not easy to keep up while still keeping her expectations in check. This is why she decided to let go completely when she could not control any situation.

"Well, I am just glad that you were able to see the light. And guess what? I am so thankful for all these silly mistakes that you make and lessons that you learn because I get to learn from them without actually being stupid myself!" Satrupa pinched his nose jokingly before giving him a big, affectionate hug, knowing very well what a tough and stressful day everyone had had.

But in the silence after, Manav still felt the slightest pang of something amiss.

Moral - The true soul of a business is the good it does, even in the process of being profitable. As a rising entrepreneur, it is easy and common to lose sight of the good you had set out to do. But it is important to keep bringing yourself back to the original truth and track. Not just because it feels ethically right, but also because, if you get distracted from the original objective, uproot the aim that anchored the enterprise, it becomes vulnerable to the swaying storm of the industry and can potentially be swayed away and drowned in every passing trend and norm. This is not just bad for the business perception, but also an operational disaster. Keep a clear head, focus on the roots of your intentions, and keep an open mind to keep revisiting your actions.

Chapter 9

Being Flexible

When you're ahead in the game and have managed to establish yourself successfully, it is comforting to enjoy that safe position. Entrepreneurs who have started small, have boot-strapped, or have dived into a new segment always have to fight a lot harder to get to this position of some security, because of the whole tug-of-war dynamics.

Mainstream and conventional businesses have the luxury of a predictive trajectory and therefore, a set formula to pursue to become stable, profitable, and steady, if not constantly in growth. However, not all enterprise segments work in the simple, complacent equation.

Especially in the online space, growth and success are relative concepts. Wherever there is a constraint of stability, there is a wide scope of experimentation and development. Especially in the space of e-commerce, where the market, consumer, production, and rates are all changing so rapidly along with the trends and behaviour, there is no such thing as a stable state. The sooner this is learned and adapted to, the better, more efficient, and hardcore evolutionary system an enterprise's environment can absorb.

However, there's a thin line between flexibility and frivolousness, something that entrepreneurs struggle to understand and balance, especially in the phase of foundation, where every step has a momentous impact, both positive and negative.

Manav was steady and wise in learning his lessons, just as he was quick in making mistakes. During his encounter with Ram and understanding his story, Manav understood the significance of identifying the signs of a mistake and correcting them even before they happen. He had also understood that taking the honest and simple path was generally the easiest solution to all problems.

Although Manav usually made a lot of mistakes, he seemed to get away with most of them, always getting to take away a lesson, thus balancing out the harm done by the value that the lessons brought to him in the long run. The good thing, however, was that he was open-minded and ready to reflect, eager for feedback, and responsive to a new environment. It was this strength that had been saving him through the dips and curves of his entrepreneurial journey all this while.

However, the space of e-commerce was fast changing, and if he did not match up to the changing norms, he would soon find himself in a ditch that would be hard to rise from. Ever since the last convention organized by Avatar, where Manav had averted a major tragedy and potential self-destruction by coming clean to his clients, he had managed to deliver one of the best and finest products Avatar had churned out in the space of e-commerce.

As expected, Satrupa, who was always after his life to give him more content for brand building, jumped with delight at this news and was in the process of churning out a wonderfully romanticized story of the rising of the phoenix from its ashes.

As a part of the media campaign, she was interviewing several clients who had been very happy customers with Avatars. The twist was that she was adding the whole dramatic angle of struggle that had gone behind the Avatar scenes to deliver that packet of success. This recipe of success mixed with struggle, this candid, honest backside story with the front face glory, was something that drove the media mad with appreciation.

"Satrupa, you have truly outdone yourself this time!" Ved was all praises after coming back from the last virtual press conference of the week. Although the coronavirus had begun to show signs of containment in different parts of the world, India was still being cautious with its approach towards movements and accessibility, simply because it did not have enough resources to accommodate a large-scale healthcare system if everyone fell sick at once.

Therefore, the lockdown, although being lifted in bits and pieces, was still being very strongly endorsed. Because of this, most of the daily professional affairs were still being conducted online. It was only once in a while, in dire need, that people were stepping out.

"Besides," Manav would say, like a man who had complete confidence on his study and understanding of the changing scenario of the digital world, "Even if the pandemic is completely under control in the next few months, the lockdown has been around for so long that it now seems to have become the new normal," Satrupa was also in agreement.

Manav and Satrupa sat side by side on the couch, working on their laptops but often conversing on things both professional and personal. It had become almost a norm for them. Whenever they wanted to get away from the hectic space, Satrupa would come over to Manav's house, which had a little office space in one corner, and the two of them would work together, taking turns to make tea or coffee.

It was their version of a vacation or date, in between their calls and endless documentation, and ideation sessions. "Look at us, for instance. Aren't we completely productive but still so comfortable in this work-from-home scenario?" Satrupa only smiled and threw an empty bottle at him. "Yes, please get me some water as I get comfortable attending these relay calls. I am almost regretting having run the campaign," she joked.

But the luxury of humour and comfort did not last very long. Something had gone wrong, and the Avatar team was not prepared for it at all! There had been endless queries coming in over the last few days. The clients who were working on the newly synchronised payment gateway on their mobile phones were getting complaints from their customers about the failure of the gateway.

"So many customers have had their payments rejected and money stuck in a transaction. Do you know, our sales have dipped by 30 percent in just one day!" One angry client had called Manav, skipping all steps of the managers and representatives. Things were going awry, and there was still no conclusive analysis from the tech team.

"That's just one client talking. Do you know I have 73 registered complaints from clients? The rest may be some who do not have daily payment access, but when they do access it, our floodgates will open!" Ved was making the obvious point to the team.

The sales team, customer team, marketing team, and tech team were all present for this discussion, trying to figure out, first of all, what was wrong and, second, how this could be fixed.

"We are reaching out to our customers, giving them a complimentary extension of membership. We have even sent out gift hampers to their customers," Satrupa was talking on behalf of the entire marketing team.

"Even though this is a perfect PR disaster, we are trying to control any news that may spread. Sending out some distraction story is also an idea we are working on," Manav was already shaking his head halfway through the conversation.

"This is not a wise solution. No one is a newbie. Our partners and clients will know that we are trying to bribe them into forgetting the mishap. As an immediate response, that's just stupid." Manav was categorical in his response.

According to him, this was a solution that should be offered once the payment gateways have been fixed. "Before that, it's just us smiling stupidly at our clients, asking them to let go."

He made a lot of sense. But the next steps were going to require a new set of eyes, clearly.

"I think we have become a little too complacent and self-praising," he stated. He continued, "No offence meant, this includes me as well. I am going to look for a consultant with business strategy acumen, someone who can catch the nerve of this issue and prevent it from happening in the future."

Manav had already begun scanning his list and looking at his network for a possible candidate. He firmly believed in hiring people whom he knew or who came from references of those he knew very well. It was time to tap into his network and get the dice rolling.

"Hey, Arjun, I need a lot of help. What was the name of that guy who got you out of the ditch when one of your products had failed right after launch?" Manav raised a thumbs up to everyone in the team, with a smile, gesturing for them to cheer up and that they would find a solution as he walked out of the room to talk to his colleague and now a good friend, Arjun, the founder of a start-up to facilitate business acquisition.

The call went on beyond just the point of transaction, as did most of Manav's connections. He had a way of being friendly and comforting to people, which is why they felt like engaging with him, keeping in touch, and throwing in any favour. Manav did the same for anyone who came along, never expecting anything in return.

"What's the point in that? I don't remember who it was, but someone said something that circulates in the start-up circle quite prominently- Keep working, keep fulfilling your duty, never bother too much about the results or the fruits of your work." Manav would explain to Ved whenever his generosity was met with objections from his friend.

"Hello, yes, I was expecting your call. Arjun told me about what's going on at Avatar..." A calm and almost cheerful voice was speaking on the other side of the screen. The video was switched off so Manav couldn't tell what Krishna looked like, except that he had seen a photograph on one of his online profiles, and he couldn't get this uncanny resemblance with someone else he had met recently out of his head!

"Thanks for helping us out, Krishna. As you would understand, we are in a bit of trouble here." Manav had explained in great detail the situation of Avatar, of payment stuck, and clients falling apart. "It's no favour, Manav, you know that. I am a consultant, you are using my services, and we are both going to benefit from one another. That is the way things function!" Krishna exclaimed in a charming voice.

The discussion went on about how the crisis had started almost a week ago now, and things had still not gotten back into shape. The meeting concluded with Krishna assuring him that he would look into every detail and come up with a solution.

"Have you spoken to Radha yet?" Krishna asked before ending the conversation. When Manav responded negatively, Krishna made a note on his calendar to connect the two.

"She is my partner, and she handles all customer satisfaction domains. I will ask her to get in touch with you guys and help you do an evaluation for the happiness index of your customers. That will help to determine a more generic understanding of the services rather than just this specific issue."

Manav was grateful for any kind of help he could get right now.

It did not take the mastermind long to dive nose deep into Avatar's business. He went through several systems, backend, payment gateway. Krishna was in the habit of reading a lot. Whenever an issue came to him, he read all angles, research papers, articles, news, everything that was ever mentioned around it. Ever since this payment issue had come up, he knew there was some little detail that had slipped his mind.

"I am also looking into tracing the pattern of these records of complaints. This is giving me a good understanding to see that only a specific category of consumers has been raising complaints. That means that the problem is very focused and once we have figured out the roots, it won't be a very wide issue to resolve," Radha explained.

She was amazingly meticulous in her research. That was one takeaway from Radha, if there were lessons to learn. She was the epitome of dedication and devotion. Whenever she committed to something, she stood by it, no matter what the circumstances. This is exactly what happened with Krishna as well.

"Did you know Krishna and Radha used to be engaged once? It did not work out, but their partnership is eternalised. Radha is still as committed to Krishna and the business as she was on the first day. I guess that's why the two are inseparable as partners." Satrupa spoke so fondly of Radha that Manav was compelled to stop doing whatever he was doing and hold her hands.

"It's inspiring, isn't it? Just as inspiring as your love for me." His words made her smile. The duo indeed felt lucky to be with each other against all odds.

Once all data had been analysed, Krishna dialled in from his office to connect with the finance team that would manage all payment gateways and make sure the cyber compliance was in place.

"I was going through the filters put here and there, that make sure payments cannot be directed to third-party platforms, and that's when it struck me," Krishna looked more amazed than pleased with himself. "The crashes had started at a time that seemed absolutely random, with no obvious change in the system or the codes. What we did not see is that right then, a small but significant change had been made in small transactions for digitally transferred money."

He continued, "Now, if you noticed, this was only happening with clients who have e-commerce services for budget products. None of your large transaction-enabling businesses had this issue!"

Manav was flabbergasted. The policy change had been announced a week ago, exactly a day before the crash! "What stupidity was this?" He couldn't really put a finger on anyone because this had been a huge miss on his end, too.

"Never regret lessons, my friend. This was easy and correctable. All you have to do is convert pre-paid orders to a post-paid page, which, after placing the order, will take you to a separate payment page, making it all register as a post-paid purchase."

Manav made the calculations and the algorithm in his head and turned around to Ved. When he received a nod, there was a sudden, relieving smile on his face. "And by doing this, we will not be doing anything illegal? Unethical?" His doubts were coming from a good place in his heart.

Krishna smiled at him, "My advice can sound twisted, Manav, but never unethical. I always work for the larger good." Krishna patiently explained to them a little bit more in detail about how the new system would work out, what kind of changes they would have to make, and what it would mean for their clients.

After the whole fiasco had been resolved, Manav, Ved, Satrupa, Radha, and Krishna were sipping some hot coffee after a stressful sprint to reset all gateway platforms. "I guess now would be a good time for a PR stunt, Manav," Krishna smiled from behind his coffee mug.

"The gifts, discounts, stories of success, the works!"

Ved and Manav exchanged a look of humour, something that hadn't happened in the past couple of weeks at all!

"The trick, my dear friends, to stay on top of your game is not just to stay on your edge, with cut-throat competition, pacy developments, and whatnot. The real depth comes with knowledge and the wisdom to use that knowledge to your advantage. Instead of sitting ducks on a system, float like a cloud, with an abundance of knowledge and flexibility to shift around whenever there is a need," Radha mentioned casually.

The team could relate to how this could all have been avoided if they had been flexible and updated. Manav was listening and thinking with keen intent. Playing with the rim of his cup, he tapped Krishna on the shoulder.

"Since you have offered us your services and there's much to benefit from it, I would actually love your advice on some of the other areas we can evolve on," Manav said. The duo got up with their cups of coffee as Krishna gestured for a walk.

"I am glad you asked, Manav. I have been holding back unsolicited advice, but I think it will be a great idea to design your product purchase platforms more focused on mobile devices than web browsers, what with smartphone usage having shot up by 70% since your first design!"

Krishna was already making remarkable points that the team of Avatar had not even thought in the direction of, perhaps in their little complacent bubbles. He also went on to suggest a few more options, so much so that Manav had to actually take out his phone to record the conversation, there was so much he would forget!

"Another thing you should be focusing on is bringing out the illusion of discounts and user base. It's like giving out a sale without a real sale. When you create a fear of missing out amidst your client, show a sign of excessive demand and short supply in your sales pitch, you elevate your position... let's discuss this over another cup of coffee, another time."

There was a lot in here, between the discussions of Manav and Krishna, that was changing the perception of what is good and what is not.

"You have to look at the larger picture, Manav, seek the larger good. Not everything is deceit, nor a straight line between black and white. Whenever you get stuck on questions that don't have clear answers, ask yourself this: *What will happen if I don't do this?* And whether the benefit of doing it is greater than the harm of not doing it. You will have your answer."

Krishna was not just talking about being world-wise. He was also showing Manav the path of being flexible in an evolutionary way.

"Imagine if you were not offering a customisable product, if it had one blanket form and cost for all clients. Do you think you would have been able to cater to the small businesses or survive on low profits, on the other hand?"

Manav could see what his companion was trying to explain. "But will being flexible not hamper the kind of results I am seeking? Won't that hamper our projected route, if we keep swinging in different directions?" Manav had a legitimate concern.

He had seen founders lose focus, companies break down because of no order in their system. "I am not saying don't be honest and true to your core value and product. All I am saying is, be open and flexible to keep evolving as time and trends change. Say, for example, the thought about moving to a more mobile-centric platform is definitely the need of the new consumer, but you have not been open to looking at a different model. In your core design, there has been no flexibility for change. That is what needs fixing."

The more Manav thought about it, the more he was determined to reflect on all the things they had not worked out. "We designed a model and stuck to it. So many competitors have come in since, replicated the model, and moved on. No wonder it looks like we're losing our edge!"

Krishna nodded with his all-knowing smile. "You have a rising competitor, his name is Kans. He has been eliminating competition with one simple rule. Wherever there is an exhibition or conference, he manages to change the order of events and pitch right before his competition comes in. He copies and manipulates their ideas and pitches them right before them, rendering the competition useless in a second position." Krishna went on to explain that Kans would generally get to know all about a start-up's strategy by sending his agents, who acted like demons in disguise, to get to know the secret of the other organisation.

"They show up as clients, consumers, auditors, even!" Manav had heard about Kans, but he had come across as such a sober person, it had been hard for Manav to imagine that Kans could do any harm. "So what did you do about him?" He was simply curious.

"Well, I first gathered as much knowledge as I could about his business, using his own tricks. Around the same time, I knew there was a change in the norm with a high-tech delivery agency launching its roots in India. I knew this would massively commodify online purchase plans for those who wanted to work with subscription models. I asked the clients I was consulting with to keep this news under cover and portray a completely different strategy up until the time of their new announcement at the e-commerce expo. All I had to do then was make Kans believe that we were going ahead with a certain strategy, trying but failing to keep it under the wraps." Krishna explained how the expected happened.

Kans went ahead and designed a model based on Krishna's projected idea and presented it at the expo, building his base with potential clients. "We then pitched our actual model, introducing the news of the launch and partnership with the delivery giants. That made Kans crash like a castle of ice. The rest is history."

Krishna smiled, watching Manav, fascinated by his strategy. He reinstated the fact that flexibility was a luxury that could only be afforded if you had complete and utterly confident knowledge about a subject.

"Only then will you be able to manoeuvre your way around its pits and ditches," Krishna said. He continued, "Otherwise, it will backfire so bad, you will wish you hadn't experimented at all."

There was a lot of learning in the last couple of weeks, mostly around keeping up to date about the latest developments and staying in a constantly evolving mode. Manav thanked Krishna for his time and proceeded to go back to his team, not just for the conclusion of this issue but also for fixing orientation and strategy for the long run.

Moral - After a constant state of fighting and struggle, when startups reach a state of some steadiness, there is a high risk of satiation that can affect the long-term growth of the company. In the e-commerce space, when things are constantly evolving based on the market, users, tech, policies, and change in environment, if your start-up does not strongly incorporate and endorse a constantly growing and evolving culture, it is very easy to be trodden and thrown behind in the race.

Keep up with the pace of the latest development, know your subjects in the industry with great depth and accuracy, and keep your mindset in tune with the larger good. That way, you are not only being super flexible in growth but also focused and confident with a singularly dedicated direction for your success, the success of your vision and mission, imbibing your true values, while staying attuned to your environment and its many changes.

Chapter 10

Creating a Culture of Love and Peace

Imagine a scenario when the world has become your home. In a space where your dreams have come true, your business is a success, your client base is on a constant rise, and your product has found enough popularity to overshadow any negative PR. Looks like you're all set. How does that feel? Almost like this is the best place to be in, right? Wrong! As an entrepreneur, you are responsible not just for your product and services, you are also for a large network of people who are employed and served by your organisation.

Just like you would be treating your tech, software, and hardware, clients, and media, with respect and attention, the team that works on building your organisation is also immensely deserving of the same care and incentive.

However, focused and stressed about the world outside the organisations, leaders often forget or de-prioritise giving the same attention to the within the organisation. Not only is it unfair, but also operationally caustic and lethal, and can lead to slow, undetected but methodical deconstruction of the entire microcosm of the enterprise.

Of course, there are firefighting techniques that will help repair some parts of the damage. But if the core is once ruined, there will only be so much to do! Manav had reached a stage, after a plethora of struggles, where he found himself feeling confident and satisfied with his work.

During the last convention, he had taken Krishna along to connect him with some of the most influential business leaders of the world. The lockdown had gradually opened up, and although the online culture and remote working continued as an efficient and cost-effective way to work, gatherings, conventions, and events happened every now and then, allowing for physical and personal interactions around the world.

This hybrid style of working had suited Manav and his team very well, making it easy for them to work remotely when needed and travel for events and business development, sales pitches, whenever necessary. Also, with Krishna's guidance, Manav had managed to prepare a deck that appealed to the target audience.

"You will not speak the same words to explain the same thing to different age groups of people, right?" Krishna had guided him to rethink his sales strategy: "Then why would you use the same deck for a different set of clients?"

He helped him walk through every segment of the audience, which got a much higher success rate for the Avatar's sales team. With better exposure and funding, it also got easier for Manav to expand his team and another branch in Mumbai to facilitate the high-potential zone.

"Listen to the pulse of your users. They want someone who cannot just give them the tech, but also take them through a simplified process of absorbing it. If I were in your place, I would set up a customer facilitation team whose only job would be to secure the client's ease and happiness for the after-sales experience," Radha had concluded on their call, leaving an open-ended suggestion for Manav to follow.

When actions were going to follow this advice, there was going to be a lot more on Manav's plate than he had imagined.

With the setting up of a new division, diversifying into post-purchase services, and simply increasing the team strength to almost double, Manav did indeed have his plate full. But not just with the workload, orientation, and streamlining operations, it was also cumbersome to live out of a hotel room for 2 months straight, to keep coordinating between two offices, forgetting the missing nuts and bolts he had begun to take for granted in Vaikunth's establishment, and whatnot!

Manav had always considered himself to be a patient man, but he was finding it difficult even for his mind space now.

"I don't know Satrupa," he complained like a little boy. Satrupa was his comfort, go-to spot. "It's just a lot of chaos in the mental space. Managing two places, pinning problems, and more importantly, getting everyone to be on the same page is a little too taxing!"

Satrupa knew the concern very well. Although she was in Vaikunth and had been away from Manav for almost two months now, she was trying to put her grievances aside, once again, for the larger good of Avatar. She knew very well that this was not a time for ephemeral emotions, but a good opportunity to test her patience and understanding of the situation.

"Manav, I think this is a great test for you to see how well you can do and also a wonderful example you can set for your team," she tried to encourage him.

"However, there's something else that you should consider at this stage." She had been managing the Vaikuntha branch with Ved and handling the human resource angle of things.

"In this whole transition of double pressure and performance, it is your team that has been the spine of all success, and right now, more than any other time, they deserve support and appreciation."

Satrupa was right, Manav knew it very well. His team had been working overtime and going above and beyond their specified roles to make sure that the expansion and transition work well.

However, there was a deeper factor in play here than such a feel-good factor with the team members. In Manav's weekly sync-up with the team, he could see the tension and friction between teams. He couldn't put a finger on it, but he knew that something was a little off.

"Is everything alright, Ved? It felt like sandpaper in there!" Manav asked Ved after the virtual meeting had over.

Ved had been meaning to talk to him for a while about it. "Manav, a lot of people are not happy with a lot of things going on in the background. You promoted a few people to the new office and brought some new members onto the team without discussing with the senior members. That has caused a little bit of disturbance and edginess. Not because growth is an issue, but also because there was no transparency in what was going on."

Manav had not considered this at all. He had been so busy building up the platform that he had completely removed himself from the internal dynamics of Avatar.

"It is natural to cause a disruption, Manav. They have been working overtime, under a lot of stress and frankly, without much appreciation," Ved said.

Manav felt like someone had changed a painting upside down! This perspective changed his perception of the situation altogether. All this while, he thought that he was the one who had been struggling and burdened, cribbing to Satrupa or seeking respite. But he had not realised the extent of turmoil it must be causing for those who were not as deeply invested or profited, but still immensely affected by this flux.

"I had not realised what a self-centred boss I must be coming off as to them, people. No wonder, this is making way for internal politics and clashes!" Manav signed off that night thinking about the next steps he would have to take to resolve this issue before it started breaking down the composition of Avatar.

That night, while scrolling through his professional media platform, he came across some activities that appealed to him as constitution-building of the organisation.

"I have to explore who has been preaching these methodologies! Such a constructive and balanced approach to organisation development!" He kept mumbling that Satrupa was busy trying her hand at digital painting. She did that sometimes.

When she wanted to clear her head and take a break from work, she just hung out with Manav without really interacting with him or talking much. She would simply work on a sketch and keep improving it in every session. This way, she stayed productive but at the same time earned herself a much-needed mental break. Manav researched more and more to reach the source of one of the sessions that had a recording online. It belonged to some guy called Siddhartha, with an online profile called Buddha.

Buddha seemed to be the leader of an organisation called Dharma and provided workshops in an ethical and balanced culture setting, and promotion in organisations across verticals. Buddha seemed to be very popular, especially in Southeast Asian countries where a culture of the central path is very strongly endorsed, as opposed to the West.

Manav, who was now driven to take a quick and concrete action, reached out to Buddha with an introductory email, asking to connect to see if there was a possibility of working together. And as soon as he was done sending in the email, he called Ved late into the night.

"Have you heard of this guy called Buddha?" Ved, the all-knowing library, had, of course! "Yes, he is based out of Sarnath, I think. He and his team are excellent preachers and practitioners." The validation coming from Ved was very comforting, in the middle of the night, after which Manav finally got some sleep.

"Hello, everyone! Sorry for not being available in the last few weeks!" Manav looked and sounded a lot more excited and positive than he had in the last month or so. This, in itself, was a game changer for his team's energy.

"Yeah, Manav, we miss you here!" Jokes and small talk flooded the room. It was once the ice had been broken that Manav decided to breach the subject.

"People, I have something very important and critical to share with you. We have a major project to work on; we have to revamp something."

The team unanimously turned their smile into frowns. They were already going through overtime, and now a new overhauling was the last thing they wanted!

Before this completely depressed the room, Manav added, with a twinkle in his smile, "Don't worry, folks, this is no additional work. Only the way you guys feel will be changed now, hopefully for the better. I know everyone has been working above and beyond, and I owe you a great deal. Which is why there's something awesome waiting for you the weekend after next!" Manav explained his idea of the first Avatar retreat, on the occasion of their annual day, which had never been considered last year because priorities were very different.

He had gotten in touch with Buddha's colleague and partner, Yashodhara. She had been managing all domestic and internal projects for Dharma, and although she was quite disconnected from Buddha, the online presence, she had been a great associate of Siddhartha. It was that healthy equation that still helped to keep the cycle of internal and external matters going smoothly. "Yes, you're lucky that just the weekend opened up for his availability! I think he will be very happy to talk to you and discuss the next steps!" Yashodhara had been a kind and patient woman who, although always in the background, had been a great contributor to Buddha's success.

"I don't know how she does it! We have been going crazy with our stress, distance, and lack of contact in just two months, while living in two different cities," Buddha exclaimed.

Yashodhara gave up her family life, her relationship with her husband, just so that the man could pursue his dreams and follow the path that inspired him to change many professional cultures. Later, when Satrupa, Manav, and Yashodhara would become really close friends, having worked on a few assignments together and travelled together, they would also discover some of the deepest struggles of such a relationship.

"I would never call it failed, though," Satrupa would tell them later.

"It is a relationship evolved to another level of existence. There is utter and honest acceptance and honesty in what Siddhartha had to do to become Buddha, to answer to his true calling. And although there were times when it made me bitter with the feeling of abandonment, I learnt to grow and understand how valuable it is to find one's true calling and how blessed it is to be able to pursue it or to see it pursued," Yashodhara's words had made Manav and Satrupa look into each other's eyes with deep respect and love, with recollections of the struggles their relationship had been through because of their professional aspirations. And yet, they had, amidst all their chaos and ups and downs, found respect and understanding for each other's crests and troughs.

Yashodhara had patched them with Buddha's client servicing team, and finally, they were getting on a call with Buddha to see what the gung-ho was all about. When they logged into a personalised video conferencing platform, it greeted them with a soothing chime of the Tibetan bowls. The interface had a running waterfall in the background! It felt like Ved and Manav were immediately put at ease.

When Buddha logged in, his eyes half open and his lips turned into a subtle smile, a lot of Manav's discomfort was put to ease right away. "Gentlemen, good evening. It is an honour to finally get to meet you." Buddha spoke in a calm but serenely influential tone. He had been briefed in detail about the origin and situation of Avatar and had eagerly jumped to meet its founders and help out.

"I feel blessed to find an opportunity like this. To work with people who are bringing about the real change, helping people at the grassroots level!" Buddha was cheerful and deeply serious all at once, with a certain appeal that attracted people to listen to him. They discussed how the expansion had been causing a lot of stress and politics in the organisation, taking away a lot of efficiency.

Buddha nodded knowingly, perfectly understanding where this was headed. "Yes, that's where Dharma comes in. We follow a simple formula of balance for any orientation in an organisation that could be struggling to set right its inner culture. I also see a huge potential in increasing the inter-departmental strength and communication here to help with your efficiency issue. I understand you have an intervention platform in mind?" Buddha had thought the whole thing through, and it appeared like he just needed a nod from Manav to take complete control of the situation and dive in.

Weirdly enough, it did not come across as either strange or unsafe from someone they barely knew. Ved explained about their retreat plan and set some expectations to get the dice rolling.

He said, "Maybe to clear out some tension amongst the new hires and the old ones, and to set a precedent that encourages a healthier relationship in the team is what we are aiming for."

They continued to discuss the nitty-gritty of the process, and Buddha took them to the basic and most conceptual understanding of the problem.

"There is no point treating symptoms unless you know the deepest roots of what is causing them. That requires patience and perseverance. More importantly, what you are looking for is the balance." Buddha spoke about how the next steps would mean designing the module for the retreat and building some tools that would be relevant for the specific purpose of their situation.

"Meanwhile, I would very strongly encourage you to spend some time with the team members, assessing their frame of mind, asserting your support and patience, and creating a sense of expectation from this retreat," Buddha signed off that meeting with a promise that left Manav and Ved eager and somewhat reassured about the upcoming retreat.

Manav did as asked by the kind-eyed man, and with some other reason, he began interacting more with his teammates, especially down the ladder, to understand their sentiments. What he sensed was a lot of fear, some anxiety, and jealousy. He would never have picked up on these behind glass doors or virtual screens had Buddha not pushed him towards one interaction.

Soon, it was time for the much-awaited retreat. It was conducted at a beautifully serene Vipassana centre on Buddha's recommendation, bordering a wildlife sanctuary and a river.

As the entire team of Avatar, all of its 104 members, old and new, stepped out of the airport shuttle, there was a sudden and obvious shift in their tone. The restlessness, eager back and forth, gossiping, and anxious impatience were replaced by long, deep breaths, a physical and mental calmness like the one that spreads into your being when you suddenly feel a cool, generous breeze on a hot, sunny day.

Buddha welcomed them all personally into the abode with his signature smile and a humble greeting with his hands folded into a namaste. After refreshing, welcoming, and settling into their rooms, Manav jumped to ask when the sessions would begin.

"Take it easy, Manav. Your team has been neck deep in work for months now. If you want to achieve success, you must aspire for balance." Buddha reassured him and sent a word out for the team to gather in the garden for a walk to the stream. As little groups of people walked along a gorgeous and adventurous path leading through the forest, and mostly fell into silent observation.

Buddha had attached a speaker to a convoy lead with each small pack to allow for easy communication amongst groups. "Isn't life's journey just like this? There are rocks and pebbles, but there are also flowers and the gurgling of distant water like hope."

This made many smile. "So you mean this hike is about to get a lot tougher? Someone spoke through the microphone, planted intentionally along with the speakers, to encourage a lot of uninhibited discussions.

"Absolutely. And I guess you can imagine what also lies beyond!"

The team huffed and puffed, struggling on some turns, helping each other out with a pull or a push. Encouraging words were heard from the speakers every few minutes. A couple of free minds also started humming a tune, sending almost everyone into a wave of music, too!

"How much longer, Buddha?" Satrupa, who had managed to twist her ankle a while ago, asked, trying to sound as patient as possible.

"Just as you think you are about to give up, remember, there's a reward waiting around the corner," Buddha answered, and his words were followed by synchronised gaps as groups poured one after another to embrace a picture of beauty they had never seen before. Before them lay a large, icy blue lake with the stream pouring into it, forming a short waterfall, explaining the enchanting gurgling sound all along.

"Is this worth all the trouble?" He smiled as he saw people rush towards the little pool of water before the lake. Even the quietest and serious ones could not help but smile as they dipped their feet at the brim. "And this is where we will have our first session," Buddha smiled as he sat down, encouraging everyone to find their comfort spots. He asked them about what they had learnt from this little hike. With a mix of responses like patience, perseverance, hope, etc, Buddha smiled and nodded at all. Adding only in the end, the significance of balance.

"When there's hard work, it is balanced with reward; when there's chaos, it is balanced with silence. But you have to choose to walk the path. Only when you do will you discover the power of this balance."

They discussed more examples of balance, especially at work.

"Generally, this balance is upset when we either lose our focus or get biased." He reiterated the significance of being a dispassionate actor in your story, with utmost sincerity, and yet, an observer's intellect.

"I am not going to rush them from one conference hall to another. They have had enough of that in the office. This is a safe space for reflection and realisation, Manav," Buddha explained to him as they walked towards the lunch buffet that everyone was already relishing after a long walk.

"You have to assess the needs of your target audience. Understand what they want and deliver to their needs first. That way, you have their faith and goodwill."

He talked to the set of people sitting around him in the diner. However, the display LCD lights flickered with the words 'faith' and 'goodwill' for the benefit of everyone else, too. Buddha talked about the universality of truth, despite its many versions.

"The truth is that everyone wants to be happy. And you only have to keep in mind that happiness can be different things for different people," Buddha projected the idea of keeping discussions open and transparent and encouraged people to shift around the room and sit to eat with people they did not gel with in the past or had had an issue with.

"Be gentle, but be transparent. See whether you can help the other person achieve their happiness." Simple, honest words between teammates began to flow.

"This would not have happened had we not let them enjoy the earlier session of appreciation, reward, and balance." He explained to Ved, who was surprised to see the set of people who had earlier been burning with friction now giving each other a chance.

After a gratuitous conversation over lunch, which really did not feel like an organised session for everyone but still worked wonders, Buddha encouraged people to go back to their rooms, rest, and write down whatever they had experienced.

"Allow expressions. Allow yourself some peace and creativity amidst all the chaos around you," he parted with this wish and greeting to everyone.

The evening was spent in some open rounds of discussions about challenges that all cadres of members felt in Avatar. Some of it revolved around being cluelessly jolted into different tasks, while some other points included workload and lack of coordination.

"Now, what if you are a trainer who earns a living by finding solutions based on people's problems," Buddha explained. "Would you see this as a hurdle or as an opportunity?"

There were a few laughs around, "Yeah, our problems will make one rich trainer!"

Buddha laughed along too. "So let us make ourselves rich today and conduct our training to solve these problems..."

Manav, who had been participating as a backbencher, walked around to sit where Satrupa had found a corner seat. "I guess this is what you wanted, darling?" He asked her quietly.

He was well aware that Satrupa was sincerely dedicated to the goodwill of Avatar and all the good it would bring in the world. She had never asked for anything for herself. But watching her right now, looking at all those smiling faces, made her smile, and this is all that mattered between the two of them. This was the balance they sought amongst themselves.

Buddha, on the other hand, was talking about a balance, demonstrating by piling himself onto a life-size scale. "And what would all these meetings and clients and salary bring for me?"

The audience responded with "luxury" and "comfort," and that made Buddha continue. "And what if neither has the time nor the people to share the luxury and comfort with?"

This was responded to with several knowing nods. "I would like you all to send messages or call your loved ones. Express about anything you like, between them and you."

As unprofessional as it seemed in the middle of a corporate retreat, it spoke volumes about the intent of the culture that Avatar was set to move towards. "Keep a balance, spend equal time and ownership with everything and everyone you love. If you do that, you will never have a reason to worry or complain."

Amidst the cheering and clapping, more such candid conversations and unconventional discussions continued. People were encouraged to join back in their comfort clothes and pyjamas after dinner for a musical night, followed by dinner and a walk under the moonlight.

This was only just the first day of the retreat, but Buddha had already worked his magic of Nirvana on many people. He was not talking about some fancy, impractical, and superficial concepts, but real-life feelings and real-life connections. That is what everyone was looking for: to be able to connect with others and to be able to be honest and safe around them.

Manav, Satrupa, and Dev submerged their own stressed spirits into the relaxing waves of the night and allowed themselves to feel free after a long time, with people whom they truly could see as valued members of their family. There was a lot to learn from this one day, to set a culture of goodwill, peace, and truth within the organisation.

Moral - For external success, internal contentment is extremely important. Similarly, in the space of enterprise,

just as valuable is the product image in the market, so is the culture and environment given and built around the people who contribute to making the enterprise. While often this is an ignored or overlooked essentiality, its ignorance can lead to disastrous deconstruction of the system and its people who have worked hard to make the name stand.

It is extremely important to set a culture of solidarity, trust, transparency, and most importantly, a balance amidst the greatest asset of your enterprise—the human resources. Not only is this the most ethical and fair way to conduct business, but it is also the most rewarding and wise way to ensure a smooth operation, healthy efficiency, flawless scaling up, and complete and honest understanding of what is going on within the company.

The significance of these factors should not be underestimated, and although they may not show any immediate or tangible economic value, in the long run, they can and will be responsible for making or breaking your enterprise. Invest in your people and promote a culture that values them and respects all of their understandings and needs.

Chapter 11

The Future

"Take a deep breath in…. relax and breathe out…"

Mellow bells chimed in the background, and a calm and soothing voice played in the creative arena of the new Avatar office. It was the golden hour of the day, and the sun was just touching the horizon.

The creative arena had been specifically designed to make the best of the natural environment in Vaikuntha. Within the office greenhouse, covered with plants of different varieties, the sunlight filtered through the glass, and amidst the many palm leaves, it kissed the face of the meditators who gathered together every evening.

Ever since Buddha's Dharma retreat last year, a lot of team members have enrolled in his meditation program. As the culture grew and started spreading a deeper impact on people's equation with one another, it was collectively decided that an hour of recharge time, dedicated to meditation, sports, and art, will be allotted every evening, where all teams in all locations will be encouraged to zen themselves.

Although it appeared to many as a weird quirk in the beginning, the trend caught on fast as more and more people started participating in the Zen hour. The only rule was that this time was not to be used in useless gossip. A couple of enthusiasts started bringing in their canvases to paint. Some brought in their cameras, and before time, the whole office had caught on to this contagious effect!

"You know, the last time my clients were here, they even joined in the Zen hour. They are now trying to introduce it in their company!"

Ved was excited to see the rippling effect. Buddha's constant guidance had encouraged the entire Avatar family to promote a culture of wellbeing and positivity, inside and out. Anytime a member felt stressed or overworked, people stepped in to support and relieve them. Manav also made sure that no one worked overtime for too long, and even if they had to, they were duly appreciated and rewarded.

It was because of these changes that several people had started taking a lot of ownership in Avatar and being more open about sharing their ideas and concepts for collective growth. A weekly scrum, also proposed by Buddha, has become a norm now where people from bottom to top share their ideas and thoughts and discuss every possibility.

"Don't be afraid to take risks or be creative. We have nothing to lose but a lot to gain," Manav would keep prompting people during open meetings.

It was a result of one such scrum when one of the interns, who had been handling customer happiness for the health segment of e-commerce, came up, scratching his head, looking a little puzzled. He had multiple calculations going on in his head, and it looked like he would burst open if he did not share something right away!

"Yes, Kapil. What is it that's bothering you?" Satrupa, who was always quick to read people, broke away from a design she was working on to address the uneasy boy. Satrupa and Manav had decided not to get married or take on familial responsibilities because they felt that they had more than enough people to share their love and care with.

"This is my family, Manav. I don't think I need anything more than working with everyone here and helping everyone grow, too," she would often tell Manav, who sometimes felt guilty for the couple not having enough time for each other.

They had a great partnership, although it was not without faults. Why should it have been anyway? They were humans who had given up a lot in their own spaces to sync up their individual and composite goals. But they tried their best to look out for each other. They looked for inspiration in whatever they could find and were always open to realising their errors and learning from them.

It was also a blessing that they had encountered some of the most insightful and influential couples around them, who had brought to them the wisdom one rarely finds at a young age. Through the imperfections, achievements, and challenges of others, they had gained a second-hand experience into couple goals, especially to match their personal and professional balance.

"Besides, it is not like we are a digital code, a software that is designed to perfection. It takes time for us to learn and unlearn, and that is a journey I love!" Satrupa would talk about their equation to media houses whenever it turned, as it almost always did, to a personal front.

It was another aspect of their balance that helped them recognise their strengths and weaknesses. Satrupa had a keen eye for evolution and creating new products, while Manav was good at handling business. This is why Satrupa led most of the scrum talks and encouraged teams to catch the pulse of the market and work in that direction. She encouraged Kapil, after watching his anxious body language, to come and sit with him and talk.

"So, you know how I have been working with the whole sector of health for client support?"

It was easy for people, especially youngsters, junior-level employees, to come and talk to Satrupa because she made them feel comfortable and listened to. It was because of this that new ideas were bounced off her every now and then, because uninhibited discussions were always welcome.

"Tell me, what do you have in mind about the health sector?"

Kapil smiled, knowing Satrupa was in listening mode. "Well, not just for the health sector, I thought of an application that could bring in a massive change in our efficiency in all the sectors."

The more detailed Kapil got into explaining his idea, the more people started gathering around him, nodding, relating to the idea, and endorsing its relevance.

"I think we can build a chatbot that, with machine learning, will be able to fulfill all the basic queries of the clients, irrespective of the scale or the time of the raised query." Kapil was talking about building an AI tool that could add to the service quality and speed of Avatar.

"There are so many questions that are pretty much the same, asked by different clients. In fact, after a point, we already know what kind of questions they are going to ask based on what stage of usage they are in with Avatar!"

Another intern, Sudha, added. And just like that, a whole jamming session with ideas began to assess how this idea could be transformed into a reality. "I think all the data of queries that the customer happiness team has as of now will come in very handy if we start with the machine learning activity right away."

Right there, there was one step covered. "Instead of having to start from scratch, we will have to start developing the code and start with the machine learning process on the go."

More interns joined in the discussion until a big crowd of really excited youngsters had turned the conference hall into a storm. There was scribbling on the board, people frantically researching on their systems, so much going on all at once. Manav was drawn to the bustle like a fly to sugar.

"What have we here?" He poked his head in out of curiosity. All of a sudden, the whole ambience fell silent. Everyone turned their heads towards Satrupa, and on receiving a subtle nod from her, they burst into another set of conversations, all at once, trying to tell Manav about what they had thought. Words like "chatbot" and "assistance" were flying around. When Manav understood, more or less, about what was going on, he asked them to settle down.

"I think it is a great idea, and I commend Kapil for having come up with this. It is so heartening to see that the next generation of Avatar is already eager and ready to build the next world Avatar!" Manav said.

He was genuinely happy to see initiative coming in with this strong sense of ownership and remembered Buddha's words when he had said, "Remember, Manav. When people start coming to you with ideas instead of following your command, know that you have imbibed a good culture for the organisation."

Not holding back, unlike his old self, Manav dived right into the ideation. "So, I have a suggestion, if you are open to it."

Receiving eager nods, Manav began explaining his idea of taking one step further from a chatbot into a virtual assistant. "If you're looking at the future, aspire for at least one step ahead of what already exists."

Manav highlighted the nature of the target audience, saying, "The most important point is to understand who wants assistance. These are people with no tech background and very little understanding of the processes. Some of them are not even equipped enough to use chatbots. What should we do then?"

He got his interns thinking, and Satrupa prompted. "What is it that people with a conventional understanding and background like to do?"

The answer was quite obvious. "They like to talk. About what is going on and what is not. That helps them arrive at solutions."

Manav smiled with a nod. "So we have to create a voice assistant that not just communicates with them, but can understand their level of worry, understanding, etc., and match that in tone and simplicity of response. We have an opportunity to build an artificial guiding persona, people!"

The next couple of months were spent on taking apart each and every component that was required of the Artificial Assistant and working on a theoretical model of its execution. While Ved and Satrupa were looking at the design and tech angle, supported by several interns and freelancers, Manav was single-mindedly trying to raise funds to enable the tech development for this. To say that this was out of their league would be unfair statement, because if there was anything Manav had learnt from all the support he had received from his nine mentors, it was that capacity is a limitless vessel and can bring about miracles, if only the right set of focus and values are applied.

"We are here to change the way e-commerce is accessed by those who are not savvy enough to handle it independently. For small businesses, who have not had a fair chance to grow, who have had the misfortune of being duped and misguided by middlemen who take advantage, we propose to put an end to the struggles of the old ideas struggling in the new world order. We propose Kalki," Manav had spoken at one of his pitches with a world-famous venture capitalist, Lakshmi.

Lakshmi had been referred to by an old mentor and well-wisher, Vishnu, who had helped Manav in several times of need. When the final call to listen to the pitch had succeeded, after almost a month of back and forth and rejections, Manav and Satrupa had revised and reconsidered aspects of their pitch, keeping in mind Krishna's lessons of being flexible and open to changes.

"Manav, in the new world order, not only is it ethical and sensitive, but also a major goodie point to make our products that are gender inclusive and sensitive," Satrupa said.

"When we think of Kalki, a male-centric artificial intelligence bot that will guide an already male-centric tech world, we exclude a whole set of female entrepreneurs who might find inspiration from a guiding female figure. When you're pitching for Kalki, make sure to pitch for the character as a gender agnostic form that can take any avatar, as per the requirement of the customer. The avatar should be customisable enough to include all races, classes, genders, and backgrounds. This speaks volumes of your sensitivity towards the marginalised section of the population, which makes a huge chunk of your desired audience," she concluded.

Satrupa's proposition made so much sense, Manav almost had tears in his eyes. Not so much because he was proud to see how sensitive and wise his partner was, but also to see that the entitlements that his own life had prevented him from seeing had been brought to notice by a very sensitive and responsible human being, whom he respected immensely. It was this, rather insightful input, that Manav incorporated in the brief the next day for the pitch.

"Now Kalki comes in multiple avatars, the most critical incorporation being of ender and diversity inclusion. Not only does Kalki cater to the needs of a target audience that may not be very tech savvy and feel overwhelmed with too much or too little information, Kalki will also be enabled with best practices guidelines, ethical decision making and flexibility to mould its language and tone based on the position and understanding of the target audience. We also plan to integrate it with augmented reality, so Kalki can show what an ideal world, the world of e-commerce space, based on the user's choice, would look like, with dummy transactions and services."

Building all of this was going to require a lot of resources. These resources would cost a great deal of money. The good thing was that no artificial intelligence had been built around this segment to cater to the needs of the masses. Which is why, when Manav pitched to the humanitarian appeal of Lakshmi, he knew he would get an appropriately positive response because not only was this service very philanthropic, but it would open up an entirely new market of the masses that could be tapped by several of Lakshmi's ventures, thus making it a scale product. It did not take long before Avatar was granted a series A funding to help develop Kalki, the avatar for the future.

"Keep me posted. I'll help you connect with some of the largest user database systems in e-commerce, which should help you purchase a variety of content for machine learning." Lakshmi concluded the meeting with a commitment of funding and to revert to Manav with the exact evaluation amount and the legalities, etc.

The work began in full swing. More people were hired, some advisors were brought on board, and hardware options were being explored simultaneously as the tech team got down to writing the skeleton algorithm of the AI. To get the correct sense and feeling of the AI, they had assigned a dummy voice and mask for the output interface. Kalki appeared when he popped with a question. At this stage, it was a mere avatar on screen, almost resembling a blue, fluid creature, which people called a genie or a Vishnu-like form.

"Of course, do not focus too much on the appearance, hardware of access for Kalki. This exercise is about testing some responses of the AI to see if ML has managed to establish enough resources for decision making." Ved was explaining to Manav as they were excited to check out the first dry run.

"Kalki, can you hear me?" said a young intern.

She was immediately addressed in a sweet, comforting tone, "Hi! I can hear you loud and clear. What's up?"

That cool and hippy tone made everyone giggle. Next, Manav addressed the avatar, "Kalki, I am looking for some human resource candidates who have signed up on the portal. Can you help?"

Kalki immediately put on a professional appearance and tone, "Good evening. I have sent out consent forms for access to profiles. Here's a list of all those who have been approved to be contacted."

Even though Kalki had not really sent out for any approvals, it was interesting to note that the criteria had registered well in the system.

"What we are seeing here is Kalki's agility based on the user profile. What we are also seeing, rather successfully, is the ability of the AI to apply decisions of 'good practices' on basic steps. Once we have set an algorithm for criteria for relative good, it gets easier for the AI to do an impact assessment and come up with a decision. However, what you see now is that it takes a considerable amount of time for Kalki to process this request," Ved explained that there was still a lot of space and time complexity to be resolved to make sure that AI did not get machine-heavy in scaling up.

"Right now, we are not even getting into the front-end, design, or hardware part of things, although another team is working on it simultaneously," Satrupa explained.

She continued, "The priority is to get the decision-making element right and extensive. This will take at least 6 months to get as close to perfection as we can project. Till then, the hardware and user interface will have been designed for sure."

A lot of resources were spent, time employed, and changes made; it took a little over 6 months to get Kalki to a stage of beta testing with its hologram avatar. They were all waiting for approval of the timeline from the many VCs, linked with Lakshmi, to fit into a schedule where testing and presentation could be done. Till then, Kalki would have to continue being tested under the wraps without making any public mention or appearance.

During some of their discussions back and forth, Lakshmi would pop in random questions to understand what went into the operations of Avatar and Kalki. Manav was always set back into a reflective mood, recalling all of the journey, from more than 3 years ago now.

He would recall his struggles of getting laid off at a time when the market was really unstable. He thought of the initial phase of presumptions and mistakes that almost took him down, and the timely and miraculous guidance of his counsellors, who brought him back on the right track.

He thought of meeting Satrupa as a blessing and finding not only a wonderful companion and lover but also an associate and colleague who stood by him as both a constant critic and a reliable shoulder. He thought, with a lot of gratitude, about his friend and partner Ved, about the time when he had let Manav stay in his own house for months, after being laid off, while he developed the spine of Avatar.

All of these were not just emotional recollections for Manav but a true run-through of his journey of evolution. He had set out with a simple mission of making things work at all costs, and through various challenges and learnings, accomplishments and mistakes, he had come so far ahead in the game, so as to be building a path-breaking tool to change the future.

He had, in all, worked with and encountered ten different advisors, he liked to call them avatars, since these people had come into his life like an incarnation of the larger being, to help him out, knock him back to his senses, or simply show him the right track to follow. Manav kept in touch with all of them and sought their continued guidance in all of his affairs. But more importantly, he made sure to spread his experience of their guidance and principles with everyone he came in contact with.

"That is the true purpose of life. That is the reason and philosophy behind my passion for Kalki, too," he explained to Lakshmi. "My intern may have proposed the idea as a means to make delivery of services easier for our target audience who needs simple solutions, but more than anything else, I see Kalki as a means to spread happiness and values to a world that is depriving itself more and more of that access. When Kalki is ready, and you will see that it happens soon, it will change the meaning of the world as we know it. Kalki will be able to bring success and opportunity to those who have been deprived because of the lack of privileges that a few control and enjoy. When Kalki launches, there will be no ignorance or misunderstanding, no corruption and cheating of the middlemen who take the innocent for a ride, and no more struggle to even find your footing in a society that only caters to a certain segment."

Manav's passionate monologue raised the spirits of all those who had been in the office lounge area, listening in as his voice and tone elevated. That was the one true purpose and motivation that had pulled the Avatar team together despite all their adversities. This was also the reason that despite being a somewhat new space, set by people without any pedigree or popularity, with a head-office in a small town of Vaikuntha, a place that many people had not even heard of, there were well-accomplished and educated employees who partnered to work with the team as interns, part-timers, advisors or consultants in whatever capacity was required.

Several people on the team had left their glamorous jobs in big cities of the world to come and work for the Avatar family simply because it set a culture of value and motivation. The attrition rate of Avatar had gradually dropped to a very low number, exemplary for the industry, and the happiness quotient, often assessed by internal and external audits, was universally high. In a world where corporations were looked at as commercial, money-making factories with cut-throat competition,

Avatar enjoyed a culture of belongingness, creativity, and transparency. Their creative arena had been featured in some of the most popular journals and magazines of the world and had inspired many other organisations to set the same benchmarks.

Manav would now be invited to talks in universities and corporate workshops. He always made it a point to give due credit to what he fondly called his Avatars, to Satrupa, his conscience, and Ved, his strength.

He imbibed, practiced, and preached all of the lessons he had learnt from his counsellors and went on to write a book about it, which he advocated as a tool of guidance for startups who were beginning their pulse from humble sources. It was, after all, his duty to continue propagating the stories of his Dashavtara to bring the miracles to the others.

Moral - Finding a culture in an organisation that promotes and respects ownership leads to unimaginable potential for growth and innovation. When there is dialogue and open space for communication, only then can you expect the values to build and be exercised. Once that has been achieved, it will help to keep your eyes and ears open to observations, insights, and ideas that come from all levels in the organisation without underestimating or overwhelming any level of the hierarchy.

When in a stage of growth, think of the future. Think five steps ahead of where you are right now and build for that level of accomplishment. However, never forget your target audience and always stick to their relevance, guided and governed by the foundation principles of your start-up. One way to step forward is to keep an eye on the past. The lessons learnt, mistakes made, and accomplishments earned in the past can work as a solid and reliable set of thumb rules to follow.

Staying humble and working for the larger good, no matter what sector and segment you work for, will always reap good results for you and your entrepreneurial family. Thus, keep

a very open mind about the past, stay inclusive about the future, and keep an open mind to evolution as it may come as an opportunity or even as a challenge.

As long as you keep yourself surrounded by a good and sincere set of people and focus on constructive additions instead of destructive criticism, no hurdle in the world will turn around to become a stepping stone for your glory. Look out for the 'avatars' who are bound to appear in your life and your business with their experiences and insights that will help you become better, both at a personal as well as an entrepreneurial level.

Acknowledgements

Every book is a journey of reflection, resilience, and realization—and this one has been particularly special. It would not have taken shape without the support, guidance, and belief of many incredible people and institutions.

First and foremost, I would like to express my deepest gratitude to Om Books International, my publishing home, for believing in my voice and vision. Your commitment to quality storytelling and author collaboration has made this journey truly fulfilling.

A heartfelt thank you to the editorial team, Shantanu da, and Rhea, whose sharp insights, patience, and guidance have helped shape this manuscript into its finest form. Your meticulous attention to detail and unwavering encouragement made all the difference.

To Suhail from Book Bakers, thank you for being the bridge between ideas and opportunities. Your unwavering support, strategic guidance, and literary wisdom have been invaluable throughout this journey.

To my family, your constant love, support, and patience continue to be the foundation upon which all my work stands.

Thank you for giving me the space to dream and the strength to deliver.

To the countless readers, entrepreneurs, dreamers, and disruptors I've met along the way, your journeys and voices echo through the pages of this book. You inspire me to keep writing with purpose.

And finally, to the divine force that continues to guide me—you are the silent partner in every chapter I write.

As I release this book to the readers, I do so with the heartfelt hope of it becoming a bestseller, reaching those who need it the most, and sparking new beginnings in many lives.